Let the Children Speak

Let the Children Speak

A Psychological Study of Young Teenagers and Drugs

Patricia K. Light
Harvard University and
Powell Associates, Inc.

Lexington Books
D.C. Heath and Company
Lexington, Massachusetts
Toronto   London

Library of Congress Cataloging in Publication Data

Light, Patricia K
  Let the children speak.

  Bibliography: p.
  1. Drugs and youth—United States—Case studies. 2. Adolescent psychology. I. Title. [DNLM: 1. Drug abuse—In adolescence. WM270 L723L]
  HV5825.L47   362.7'8'2930973   74-313
  ISBN 0-669-92676-0

Published simultaneously in Canada

Printed in the United States of America

International Standard Book Number: 0-669-92676-0

Library of Congress Catalog Card Number: 74-313

To My Mother

Table of Contents

List of Tables

Preface

As a graduate student at Harvard, I had a number of outstanding training opportunities. They enabled me to see for evaluation—and frequently for treatment—many adolescents and their families. Because the evaluation process required the participation of both parents and was carried out over several visits, I had a chance to "get inside" these families and to establish strong working relationships with them. They trusted me as a helper and were willing to talk openly.

In the late 1960s more and more children and parents talked about drug use. The parents were anxious, suspicious, angry, or just plain puzzled. Many children were "doing drugs" a lot.

From my readings in psychological theory and practice with older adolescents, I felt as if I had some understanding of how and why they were using drugs. But the literature did not say much at all about young teenagers and I was curious about them.

Until recently I often felt that early adolescence was a forgotten topic in psychology. Differentiations between what it is like to be 13 versus 17 seemed to be all too infrequent. I believe there are important psychological differences between early and late adolescence and this is why, given the relative absence of existing studies, I decided to look into drug use by young teenagers. I wanted to understand why some of them became involved with drugs and why others did not and, most importantly, what this behavior meant —psychologically speaking. My work as a consulting psychologist provided me with ready access to young teenagers. The result is this manuscript. I look forward to sharing what I know with you.

Patricia K. Light

Cambridge, Mass.

Acknowledgments

I wish to express my thanks to the many people who were instrumental in the preparation of this work:

To Dean K. Whitla, Paul A. Walters, Jr., and Norman A. Sprinthall for their invaluable help as advisors and critical readers of my doctoral dissertation, which led to this book.

To Douglas H. Powell for his friendship and colleagueship at every stage of my work.

And most of all to my family—to my dear husband, Richard, who has always been my most ardent supporter, in this and many other enterprises. His love and encouragement, critical commentary, and his many hours of babysitting for little Jennifer and baby Sarah, truly made this work possible.

Finally, to Connie Garguilo and Vera Montani, our wonderful friends, who gave endless hours of love, devotion, and play to Jennifer and Sarah, so "Mommy can write her book." Many thanks.

1 Introduction

Marihuana was a subject of extravagant social controversy even in ancient times: there were those who warned that the hemp plant lined the road to Hades, and those who thought it led to paradise.[1]

Widespread use of marijuana and other mind-altering substances, especially among young people in the United States, is an issue that continues to provoke vehement debate. Since the mid and late 1960s the public has become increasingly alarmed about "the drug problem." To quote the official report of the National Commission on Marihuana and Drug Abuse (hereafter referred to as the National Commission): "The typical sequences of 'a national problem' have resulted: exaggeration, polarization, and the inevitable demand for a solution."[2] That a commission needed to be appointed in 1970 tells us that the use of drugs had reached crisis status in the mind of many Americans.

People have been aroused for a variety of reasons. There are those who disdain the use of anything solely for pleasure. Some see drug use as one symbol of the alienation of the young. Others feel that the passivity resulting from drug use is in direct opposition to the American tradition of activity and achievement. In any case, we are left with the impression that never have things been so bad. A psychiatrist, Sidney Cohen, decries this viewpoint as a myth, explaining, "It betrays a profound and potentially disastrous ignorance of the history of man."[3]

This book will not depolarize the issues raised by young people taking drugs; nor will it disarm or refute either side. We shall not attempt to judge the effectiveness of specific drug education and prevention programs; nor is it our intention to make moral judgments about the question of drug use and abuse. We hope, rather, to help our understanding of drug use as a psychological phenomenon. By studying a small but interesting group of young teenagers, 12 to 15 years old, in considerable depth, we can learn a great deal about

1

how they view drugs—about what drug use does and does not mean to them. In this way, together with data from their parents, we can place the decision to use or not to use drugs in the context of family background.

To understand the recent spread of the use of marijuana and other substances, and to place present usage in some perspective, we will explore some young people's motivations for using drugs and also find out something about these people. We shall try to place the decision in the framework of early adolescent development.

Remarkably little is known about the psychology of drug use by students. The preponderance of investigations have used as subjects *only* that small proportion of students who are seriously disturbed by it. Those who are *not* psychologically disturbed seem to be viewed as much less interesting. If one accepts the assumption that all drug users are not psychologically disturbed, one has to examine motivations for drug use in the light of a theory of *normal* adolescent development—a theory that acknowledges the importance of existing social conditions.

The study to follow concerns eight children—five drug users and three nonusers. We shall analyze the process of drug-taking as it develops, and the variables associated with use or nonuse.

Chapter 2 briefly reviews the research findings on student drug use. We see that data on young high school and junior high school users are surprisingly scarce. The data that are available come primarily from large-scale sample surveys like the one conducted in "Masstown."[a] In contrast, studies of college students are more numerous and more sophisticated. In this chapter we will learn that estimates made in the late 1960s suggest that a large fraction[b] of high school students have had experience with marijuana at least initially to experience pleasurable sensations—for fun. Some studies, as we shall see, emphasize that the motives for drug use frequently change and multiply once use begins. We also learn that there is no one type of person who uses marijuana, and that many of our old notions, such as the relationship between socioeconomic class and use, have had to be revised on the basis of these studies.

Chapter 3 presents the design and methodology of my case

---

[a]An agreement was made between the author and Dr. Victor Gelineau of the Massachusetts Drug Rehabilitation Board not to identify the town, a Boston suburb, by name. I have chosen to call it "Masstown."

[b]The National Commission cites that 47 percent of students in grades 9 to 12 have used marijuana.

studies. The subjects were not randomly selected. Therefore, generalizations between them and the American teenage population cannot be made easily. However, the interviews enabled me to obtain detailed case histories of junior high school students in a form that is rare in published literature. Combining these histories and in-depth interviews with projective test data leads to some interesting inferences.

In Chapter 4 we meet the subjects—the five users and the three nonusers. For each of them, there is a brief summary of family background and relevant school material. We learn how each of these users first became involved with drugs and why, what his first experience was like, and his pattern of use. The nonusers tell us why they do not use drugs and mention the factors that influence this decision. We hear what they think about those who do use drugs and about their future plans regarding drugs. We see how all of these young people think and feel about the broad questions of drug use, drug intervention programs, and the legalization of drugs.

Chapter 5 examines the findings to see what variables differentiate users from nonusers. One of the factors that emerges is the loneliness, the isolation that most of these young people experience. Also, we find hints of differences in the quality of mother-child relationships between users and the nonusers. And, we see that for many teenagers, initial drug use is not premeditated—it just happens by chance. This result is not widely reported. But if it is widespread, it has important implications for our understanding of why young teenagers take drugs.

Finally, in Chapter 6 we draw inferences about young people and drugs from these intensive case studies. Some general clinical impressions about marijuana as a psychological phenomenon in the life of a young adolescent precede an examination of theoretical formulations of Erik H. Erikson and Paul A. Walters, Jr., in an attempt to further our understanding of the meaning of marijuana use. What clearly emerges from looking at these young teenagers in depth is that young people use drugs for extraordinarily diverse reasons —some situational, some accidental, some personal. The use of marijuana is no longer limited to one subcategory of youth.

Notes

1. Lester Grinspoon, "Marihuana," *Scientific American*, December 221(6) (1969): 17.

2. National Commission: *Marihuana: A Signal of Misunderstanding, The Official Report of the National Commission on Marihuana and Drug Abuse*, New York: New American Library, 1972, p. 5.

3. Sidney Cohen, "The Cyclic Psychedelics," *American Journal of Psychiatry* 125 (1968): 394.

2

Perspective on Student Drug Use

What is currently known about students and drugs? Let's begin with a short history of illicit drug use in this country. Then we can examine the extent, motivation, and correlates of drug use among teenagers. Since so little is known about younger users, we include the more carefully documented comparative material on the college population. From these data we can formulate some tentative hypotheses and speculate about the drug-taking behavior of younger adolescents.

A Brief History

The drug flood was unleashed about a century ago in Western countries. The popularity of marijuana or cannabis in Europe among literary figures like Dumas and Baudelaire is well-documented.[1] "It is probable that the preoccupation of literary men of the nineteenth century with the sensuous connotations of marijuana have contributed to these qualities emerging so frequently in more recent reports by non-literary users."[2] The nineteenth century in England was beset with a serious problem of opium usage. Opium could then be easily purchased from the local apothecary. Though it is not widely known, the nineteenth century was also the time of the "ether frolics" at Harvard.[3] On college campuses, nitrous oxide (laughing gas), the primary psychedelic of the day, was considered the only genteel way to become "stoned."

Although such early instances exist, the use of drugs to enhance creativity or expand the consciousness was confined, clearly, to small, relatively isolated segments of the population. Public debate about marijuana did begin in the United States in the mid 1800s,[4] but it was not until about 1910 or so that it was first introduced into the southern part of the United States by Mexican laborers.[5] By 1920 its use among soldiers and people in port cities had increased considerably.[6] The prohibition of alcohol by the Volstead Act en-

5

couraged an upsurge in marijuana usage. By the late 1930s its use had spread to northern urban centers, but the users were still a narrow and well-defined segment of the population—primarily black and Latin American slum dwellers.[7] In New York, public concern, particularly about the use of marijuana among school-age children, led to the formation of Mayor LaGuardia's committee and to the "Mayor's Report." The report,[8] one of many, declared that there was no widespread use of marijuana by minors. During World War II, soldiers reportedly were taking marijuana, but again usage was restricted primarily to members of lower socioeconomic groups. It was about this time that marijuana was circulating among jazz musicians,[9] and began to spread in a more general way to minority groups, particularly in slums. Artists and members of the "beat" set continued to use it. Finally, marijuana moved onto campuses and into the high schools.

Amphetamine drugs and other laboratory-produced substances such as LSD did not even exist until almost the middle of this century. Little is known about the extent of early LSD use except that it seemed largely confined to members of the upper-middle class.[10] It was used primarily for therapeutic purposes, for inducing religious states, or both.

The historical literature on drug usage thus suggests that before 1960 or thereabout, drug-takers comprised a relatively homogeneous population. In recent years, however, the media have made us painfully aware that the use of drugs is no longer a subcultural affair chiefly limited to the poor or the "beat." Groups who previously had little contact with drugs are involved in present-day usage —college, high school and even junior high school students, housewives, professionals of all sorts. We are sometimes told today is no more an age of drug-taking than earlier times[11]—but most people refuse to believe this. They are clearly afraid of the social consequences, now that drug use has swept so many new parts of the population. Helen Nowlis summarizes the issues well when she says:

Man has used drugs throughout the ages to escape from discomfort and misery. It is interesting to note that in our society misery is a condition familiar to the socially and economically depressed, but also to those who are in the midst of "success."[12]

Why does Nowlis believe that young people are miserable? In the light of so many advances in technology and more comforts than ever before, how can there be such despair?

Sidney Cohen explains:

The old gods falter; the old goals seem pointless. What is left but to chemically dull the senses, or, alternatively, create new illusions, new utopian worlds? So it has been in every period of stress; so it is today.[13]

Extent of Usage Among Adolescents

Until recently there were few reliable published estimates of the extent of drug-taking among high school students. The literature on college students repeatedly points out how difficult it is to measure drug use. For several years we have witnessed concern by parents, school administrators, town officials, even students—concern about the "drug problem" that exists in their town among school-age youth. In the spirit of inquiry many school systems have undertaken surveys. But because of the low reliability of such survey data,[14] the variety of estimates, according to Samuel Pearlman,[15] often sound like a "numbers game."

There are several good reasons for the large variability in prevalence figures. First, figures on drug-taking, no matter how carefully collected, are greatly influenced by time and place. Estimates made in the late 1960s are probably out of date today—they may have been dated before the study was published. Furthermore, there is considerable variation as to the extent of drug use from one region of the country to another. California-based studies[16] of college students, therefore, offer little insight into drug usage in eastern, southern, and midwestern schools. Similarly, we cannot generalize from a study of Long Island high schoolers about the high school population as a whole.

Another difficulty in estimating drug usage is methodological. Any estimate will depend upon how we define use, both in terms of which drug and the frequency of taking. Did the experimenter look at one-time users, frequent users, chronic users? Even more important than these definitional problems, however, is the fact that few studies are based on carefully constructed random samples. If a random sample is drawn and questionnaires are mailed, a proportion of those selected usually will not reply. So we are dealing with a potential source of nonresponse bias.[17] In nearly every study prior to the National Commission survey nonrespondents were not followed up. As a result, many of the surveys can be considered incomplete at best; at worst, they are heavily biased. Samuel Pearlman[18] explains that it would be difficult to follow up nonrespondents in such surveys because of the investigator's desire to preserve anonymity. Similar problems exist in any study where the subjects are volunteers; volunteers rarely represent an entire student population. Kenneth Eells[19] expresses frank concern, warning that we must ask ourselves whether or not the nonrespondents are probable nonusers or users who preferred not to reply. Obviously, some nonrespondents may fall into each category.

Finally, some usage estimates may also be uncertain because of a problem inherent in any self-report technique—dishonesty. Ernest Harms[20] points out that many people hesitate to report the extent of their drug usage because of fears related to its illegality. Drug-taking data will then be under-reported. School systems, eager to avoid unfavorable publicity, may quash accounts of prevalence. On the other side of the scale, dishonesty may occasionally operate in favor of over-reporting, perhaps in an attempt to shock the investigators. Clearly, in studying an emotionally-charged issue such as this one, accurate data are hard to obtain.

Keeping these caveats in mind, let us trace the change in estimated usage patterns over the past ten years. The brief review of studies that follows is a guide to developments in the late 1960s.

Richard Blum and his associates[21] conducted a questionnaire survey of 5,480 students in four San Francisco high schools in 1967-68 at the same time that their major college study was also carried out. While they surveyed usage of a variety of drugs, we shall focus only on figures relating to the use of marijuana and hallucinogens. The results obtained are shown in Tables 2-1, 2-2, 2-3, and 2-4.

These data suggest that, as early as 1967, marijuana usage was quite widespread in the teenage world. A comparison between the first three schools (Tables 2-1, 2-2, 2-3, surveyed in 1967) and the fourth school (Table 2-4, in 1968) indicates that drug usage was increasing. Most striking are the reports by students of the increased opportunity to try marijuana and LSD. No figures on nonrespondents were reported—they are described as low.

Table 2-1
An Upper-Middle Class Suburban High School in San Francisco

Marijuana	Opportunity to Use It	Tried It	Use at Present
Boys	25%	16%	5%
Girls		10%	3%
No Answer		38%	6%
Hallucinogens			
Boys	17%	10%	7%
Girls		5%	1.5%
No Answer		34%	6%

Table 2-2
A Middle-Class Suburban High School in San Francisco[a]

Marijuana	Opportunity to Use It	Tried It	Use at Present
Boys	46%	31%	24%
Girls	45%	28%	19%
LSD			
Boys	32%	14%	9%
Girls	29%	13%	9%

[a]These data were obtained with a modified form of the questionnaire used in the upper-middle class high school.

Table 2-3
A Lower-Middle Working-Class High School in San Francisco

Marijuana	Opportunity to Use It	Tried It	Use at Present
Boys	23%	13%	7%
Girls	19%	7%	4%
LSD			
Boys	17%	5%	3%
Girls	18%	4%	2.7%

Table 2-4
A Suburban High School in San Francisco[a]

Marijuana	Opportunity to Use It	Tried It	Use at Present
Boys			41%
Girls	75%	55%	37%
Hallucinogens			
Boys			10%
Girls	67%	20%	2%

[a]This was the most recent study reported. The data were gathered in Spring 1968.

Another survey of high school youth, reported by both Blum[22] and Donald B. Louria[23] was conducted in 1967 in Great Neck (Long Island) High School. The results showed that 8 percent had tried marijuana, while only 2 percent had used hallucinogenic drugs. Other drugs (barbiturates, glue, cough syrup) were surveyed and an additional 12 percent reported using these substances. These findings are substantially and surprisingly lower than Blum's, considering the data were gathered in approximately the same period of time.

A survey by Price[24] in 1967 of 11th and 12th graders (illustrated in Table 2-5) in two schools in Castro Valley, California[a] yields results similar to those reported by Blum. Of students affirming LSD use, three fourths of the boys and one half of the girls admitted using it at least three times. Over 75 percent of the marijuana users reported using it more than three times. A 1968 study in suburban Marin County High School revealed that 46 percent had tried marijuana and 45 percent continued to use it.

One of the few studies incorporating data about younger children was conducted in October 1969 in a suburb of Boston, Massachusetts, which we will call "Masstown."[b] This study will be reviewed in some detail; it can serve as a prototype of a well-conducted, large-scale survey.

Designed and carried out by researchers from the Massachusetts Drug Addiction Rehabilitation Board under the direction of Dr.

[a]In the San Francisco Bay area.

[b]Unpublished data were provided with the understanding that the town would not be identified.

Table 2-5
Results of Survey by Price

	Tried Marijuana	Tried LSD
Boys	35%	15%
Girls	22%	9%

Victor Gelineau,[c] the study was one of several being conducted statewide at that time. One out of every five young people in grades 7 through 12, including students in the town's two parochial schools, were included. State Public Health Department researchers administered anonymous questionnaires. No school personnel were permitted inside the classrooms during the administration of the questionnaire, nor could they see the completed questionnaires. Of the 957 students in the sample, only one refused to fill in the questionnaire. The results indicate that, if all students in grades 7 to 12 were considered, 16.2 percent had used drugs.[d] For high school-age students the figures rose to about 25 percent; and if only juniors and seniors were considered, a third had used drugs. These figures include *only* those students who were still in school.

The study disclosed a broad spectrum of drug involvement in "Masstown." Students had used barbiturates, glue, cocaine, hallucinogenic drugs, and marijuana. A modest proportion of the students, 5.2 percent, used substances they could not even identify. What does this study reveal? That among these school-age drug users, marijuana is by far the most commonly used specific substance: 79.2 percent of users smoke it. Amphetamines are next in popularity: 34.5 percent "pop pills." The hallucinogenic drugs attract 15.1 percent of the drug-taking population. Most of the "Masstown" drug users do not stop after one use and tend to use the drugs rather often. The results are shown in Table 2-6. Examination of the data by age in Table 2-7 discloses a steady upward trend—the incidence of drug use clearly increases with age. Although statistical generalizations about other high school student groups cannot be made, systematic studies such as this one provide invaluable data to help us understand patterns in drug use.

[c]The details of this survey and the statistics were obtained from Dr. Gelineau (private communication) and from a computer print-out he furnished.

[d]The drugs investigated include: narcotics, amphetamines, barbiturates, codeine, glue, hallucinogens, and marijuana.

Table 2-6
Distribution of Drug Use Among "Masstown" Users[a]

How often have you used drugs?	
Once	23.2%
Few times	30.1%
Occasionally	28.4%
Frequently	18.1%

If frequently, how frequently?	
Every day	24%
2-3 times a week	48%
Once a week	16%
Once a month	4%
Twice a month	4%
Every 2-3 months	4%

[a]Data were obtained from unpublished computer output provided by the Massachusetts Drug Rehabilitation Board Survey, 1969.

Table 2-7
Frequency of Use by Age[a]
(figures are % of total N)

	12	13	14	15	16	17	18	19
Yes	5.2	6.0	11.3	17.3	26.1	30.0	23.2	28.6
No	94.8	94.0	88.7	82.0	73.9	69.2	76.8	71.4
Going to	—	—	—	0.7	—	0.8	—	—
Total	96	183	133	139	134	120	69	7
Percent	10.9	20.8	15.1	15.8	15.2	13.6	7.8	0.8

[a]Data were obtained from unpublished computer output provided by the Massachusetts Drug Rehabilitation Board Survey, 1969.

A survey of Massachusetts young people, conducted by the Becker Research Corporation[25] in January 1970, sampled high school students, college students, and working youths. They found that 21 percent of high school students in the state had smoked marijuana in the past year. They also examined the frequency of marijuana smoking and found that smoking pot tends to be a repeated experience.

An important study of marijuana use was conducted by the National Commission on Marihuana and Drug Abuse. The data,

Table 2-8
Use by Age-National Sample[a]

Age	"Ever-Users"
12-13	6%
16-17	27%
18-21	40%
21-25	38%

[a]The data for this table appeared in the text of National Commission: *Marihuana: A Signal of Misunderstanding, The Official Report of the National Commission on Marihuana and Drug Abuse,* New York: New American Library, 1972, p. 39.

Table 2-9
Use by Year in School[a]

Year in School	"Ever-Users"
Junior high school	8%
9th and 10th	17%
11th and 12th	30%
College and graduate school	44%

[a]The data for this table appeared in the text of National Commission: *Marihuana: A Signal of Misunderstanding, The Official Report of the National Commission on Marihuana and Drug Abuse,* New York: New American Library, 1972, p. 39.

gathered in late 1971, tell us that 24 million Americans over the age of 11 have used marijuana at least once. The commission defines them as "ever-users." While until recently twice as many males as females used marijuana, the survey indicates that the sex differential is decreasing. Age, as we might expect, is one of the most significant correlates of use. The "ever-users" are most heavily concentrated in the 16 to 25 group. Table 2-8 summarizes the evidence on use by age (unfortunately, they do not report specific data on the 14 to 15 year olds).

The commission survey also found that among those now attending school, the incidence of marijuana use seems to rise as the school level increases from 8 percent in junior high school to 44 percent in college. The use by year-in-school figures is shown in Table 2-9.

Patterns of use, according to the National Commission Report data, show that most of the "ever-users" are experimenters (take pot once a month or less). This group breaks down into 45 percent who have used marijuana but quit and 15 percent who use it once a month or less. Nineteen percent of the "ever-users" are designated intermittent (2-10 times monthly). Five percent use marijuana several times a week or once daily; these are the moderate users. The heavy users (several times daily) comprise 4 percent of the "ever-user" population. The nonresponse rate is 12 percent.

In spite of the difficulties inherent in obtaining accurate prevalence figures, the evidence was overwhelming: drug-taking among school age youth in the late 1960s was on the rise. The newspapers periodically alerted us not only that more kids were turning on but also that they were starting to do so much earlier. In an epilogue to his 1969 study, Blum reflects on the trend discerned in metropolitan centers:

What we see now is a rapidly increasing tempo. While it took approximately ten years, by our estimate, for experimentation and use to shift from the older intellectual-artistic groups to graduate students, it took only an estimated five years to catch on among undergraduates, only two or three years to move to a significant number of high school students, and then, within no more than two years, to move to upper elementary grades— although we have no sound data as yet on numbers involved in elementary schools.[26]

A prophetic note was struck by Louria in 1968 when he commented that "it seems likely that within the next 2 or 3 years, in many areas of the country, a majority of college and perhaps even high school students will have at least experience with marijuana."[27]

Motivation for Use

What are young people's motives for using marijuana and other drugs? The "Masstown" study found that, although some use stems from a desire to rebel against the adult world or to escape from it, most users report using drugs for the drug effect per se, that is, to experience pleasurable sensations. They like the way drugs make them feel and use them mainly to get "high" or "stoned."

In an article titled "Drug Use Among Affluent High School Youth,"[28] Richard Brotman, Irving Silverman, and Fred Suffet postulate several motives that, they believe, influence the decision to use drugs. The main thrust of their argument is that drug-taking does *not* imply psychological disturbance on the part of the taker. Drug use is part of the "youth scene;" in many subcultures it is expected behavior. A large number of adolescents are simply motivated by a desire to be "in"—to be a member of a particular group. Also, they tend to be motivated by the sensory stimulation inherent in drug effects and by a desire to experiment. The authors feel, too, that since drug-taking flashes a visible signal of dissent against society, it may reflect students' concern for the improvement and modification of that society. The last hypothesis is purely speculative, however.

In their survey of California high school students, Blum and his associates found that students said they used drugs to show hostility toward society, to escape from pressures, to find themselves, for religious reasons, out of curiosity, for "kicks ," to conform with an "in" group, and to increase creativity. A look at some of the students' responses suggests not only a full gamut of motives, but also the depth of feeling involved.

I think a lot of people take drugs just to go along with their buddies even though they may not want to take it.[29]

Drugs give you a chance to see nature very differently, in a really beautiful artistic way. Gives you a chance to be very creative.[30]

Before having grass, I hated my parents and home, but after, I began to see that parents have to have some authority and now I don't mind my home—I'm quite happy.[31]

Many of us need an escape hatch from the pressure of this damn Establishment—grades, money, status, college. Pressures upon pressures—you need to escape, in fact, I am getting so that I have to escape somehow or else I might have a breakdown! With all of the pressures and everything around us, can you blame us? You started this and we have to clean and fix up everything you messed up in the world. Now, if that isn't a good reason for wanting to escape—I don't know what gives. Freedom now![32]

Most authors agree that reasons for use are too various and complex for any single, simple psychological explanation.

Although Herbert Blumer's study[33] focuses on minority group and lower-income youth who use drugs, he raises several broad and provocative issues. He points out that the start of marijuana use *must* be viewed in a group context—it is the peer group or subculture that plays the largest role in an individual's decision to use drugs. He argues that most use is *not* motivated by a desire to escape reality, but rather is a means of "embracing" reality—an effort by users to get into *what they see* as the mainstream of reality. In other words, reality depends on whose eyes are viewing it. Blumer argues that no evidence to date supports the idea that "induction into drug use is an expression of a well-defined pre-existing body of motivation."[34]

College surveys confirm this idea of complexity of motives. Richard Goldstein's work[35] strongly suggests that there are even regional differences in students' motives for drug-taking. Within *one* college or university, students do not seem to use drugs for a single or even just a few reasons. Moreover, Blum[36] stresses that motives may multiply once use begins.

Why do college students and young adults use drugs? Let us look at what the major research findings are in this area.

As a graduate student in journalism, Goldstein[37] observed students on 50 campuses across the country. His data, like Harrison Pope's,[38] were not gathered from formal questionnaires, but were acquired chiefly through direct questioning of students and also, informally, by living with them. He reports that the majority of users claim they use marijuana simply because it gives them pleasure. "The rationale is as simple and dumbfounding as that."[39] Reasons other than pleasure-seeking are also given occasionally: curiosity, relief from boredom, to express rebellion, to have an intense personal experience, and to seek status with a peer group. Several researchers make an interesting distinction between "the dabbler," "the user," and "the head." The dabbler usually approaches marijuana for reasons outside the drug experience proper. For him marijuana is something daring, something that arouses curiosity, or something he does just for kicks. The user, in contrast, enjoys smoking pot, but also enjoys its ritualistic aspects—that is, the mystique surrounding the drug. "What is outstanding here is the importance of the group. . . ."[40] The heads, who form the smallest segment of the drug-taking population, may turn on alone or with a small group. For them, no matter what the initial reasons are for using marijuana, the motive to continue is entirely within the drug experience. Drugs become a new reality. These kinds of distinctions have not been made in the few studies of younger users.

In a comprehensive questionnaire survey of Cal Tech students, Kenneth Eells differentiates reasons for use of different drugs by drug—marijuana vs. LSD. His results are shown in Table 2-10.

Table 2-10
Reasons for Using Marihuana and LSD[a]

Reasons for Use	Marihuana Users Agree	LSD Users Agree
(1) Interesting experience for its own sake	33.9%	35.6%
(2) Curiosity	26.0%	10.2%
(3) Kicks	14.2%	16.9%
(4) Escape from problems	2.4%	2.0%
(5) Help with personal problems	1.6%	8.5%
(6) Social pressure	.8%	0.0%
(7) Boredom	0.0%	1.7%
(8) Others and combinations of above reasons	21.3%	27.1%

[a]Eells, Kenneth, "Marihuana and LSD: A Survey of One College Campus," *Journal of Counseling Psychology, 15(5) (1968):* 465. Copyright 1968 by the American Psychological Association. Reprinted by permission.

These results must be considered in light of the finding that most LSD users have also used marijuana. If an understanding of motivation will help in mounting campaigns against drug use, then nonusers must also be considered carefully. Few investigators have taken them in account. Eells is one of the few who has, and he has found that among nonusers of LSD, 43.1 percent cited medical or health concern as their primary reason for nonuse. Of those who did not smoke pot, 48.2 percent abstained mainly because they were not interested.

The most comprehensive study done to date on motives for student drug use was made by Blum and his associates.[41] The reasons given for marijuana use were: for self-exploration, for religious-seeking, to combat depression, for mood elaboration, to enhance friendliness, to improve or reduce sexual appetite, to avoid panic or psychosis, to enhance learning or recall, and to insulate against stimuli. Unfortunately, no attempt was made to establish a hierarchical structure of these motives. Thus we cannot say which motive is *most* powerful for *most* people. However, diaries kept by students revealed that on 75 percent of all occasions when marijuana was used, pleasure was the purpose. Nonusers are guided principally by negative considerations—fear of either bad physical effects or legal difficulties.

Norman Zinberg[42] distinguishes two types of drug-abusers—the "oblivion seekers" and the "experience seekers." The oblivion seekers are predominately members of lower socioeconomic groups using drugs as an escape from disagreeable life conditions. These are often (or used to be until very recently) the heroin addicts. The experience seekers are middle- and upper-income people who are using drugs "to embrace" life; they use a larger variety of drugs. Student users fall almost entirely into this latter category. Zinberg feels students use drugs because they are afraid of not really living or fully experiencing life unless they do. "Many experience-seekers want to extend themselves in inner and outer time and space; they strain against personal boundaries; they want *all* knowledge and feeling to be available to them. . . ."[43]

In one of the *Marihuana Papers*,[44] Howard S. Becker presents a persuasive case for the multiplying of motives that, he says, cannot occur until the individual learns to become a marijuana user. On the basis of interviews with 50 subjects, he postulates three steps in becoming a user. At first the user experiences no pleasure because he has not yet learned how to smoke a joint. Later, he must learn to perceive the effects—to identify the symptoms of being high. Lastly, he must learn to enjoy these effects.

In the course of this process he develops a disposition or motivation to use marihuana which was not and could not have been present when he began use, for it involves and depends on conceptions of the drug which could only grow out of the kind of actual experience detailed above. . . . He has learned, in short, to answer "Yes" to the question: "Is it fun?"[45]

Becker believes that the taste for these experiences is socially acquired and reinforced by a peer group. While he contends that learning to enjoy marijuana is a necessary condition for continuing to use it, he says that enjoyment is not enough to produce a stable pattern of drug use. Marijuana use, according to Becker, does *not* occur because a person wishes to escape from psychological problems with which he cannot cope. Rather, it is a pleasure-giving and recreational phenomenon.

Louria[46] argues that the major psychological[e] influence upon

---

[e]He postulates a complex interaction of sociological forces to account for general use by the population.

drug use, affecting both marijuana and LSD, lies within the peer group. Since smoking pot and "taking a trip" are primarily communal activities, many young people, he asserts, try and continue to use these substances for fear of being called "chicken" or "square"; because they are anxious "to keep up" and "go along" with the group; and, also, because they are curious. Cohen[47] concurs with these reasons, but he also includes the drug effect per se—the "high." Louria states: "Indeed, at any age at which the approbation of one's colleagues is of immense importance to a maturing but emotionally insecure individual; it takes great strength of character to reject use if a substantial percentage of the peer group is involved."[48] This view agrees with the implications of Erikson's adolescent development theory, that is, the importance of peer group identification.

In his study as a participant-observer, Pope[49] finds that most young people use marijuana and LSD for fun, not out of deep psychological need. He argues that the theory of "psychological need" for drug use springs from two false assumptions. First, that drug use is so dangerous that no one would dare use drugs unless he really "needed" to. Second, that our work ethic says that hedonistic pursuits (pleasure for its own sake) are evil and thus everything must be done for a purpose. It then follows that most people take drugs because they need to.

Pope doesn't buy this explanation. For him: "Marijuana or LSD use is very rarely the compulsive satisfaction of an acute need. Practically all users perceive taking these drugs as mere enjoyment. . . . Drug use, like driving sports cars, may of course reflect more subtle, unconscious "psychological" needs, but its primary attraction is fun."[50]

This idea of simply having fun is what many young people attest. But how reliable are such reports? Barron[51] believes that self-reports are generally unreliable because people often state their motives with little or no insight into themselves, and, therefore, into their behavior. Other investigators say that a person's statement of why he takes (or took) drugs is affected by a need to justify his previous actions. The studies of Howard S. Becker[52] and Blum[53] raise the issue of changing motives over time. Interpreting self-reports is a different business. But more about this in Chapter 3.

Correlates of Drug Use

> The typical marihuana user is usually twenty to thirty years old; he is idle, lacking in initiative, usually frustrated, often sexually maladjusted (homosexual) and seeks distraction or escape through a bogus conviviality. He almost always has major personality defects, is impulsive or otherwise emotionally unstable.[54]

This quotation describes the drug user as Goodman and Gilman saw him in 1955. Times have changed. We know now that there is no one type of person who smokes marijuana. Although there have been numerous personality-focused studies of narcotics addicts, there have been fewer attempts to investigate the characteristics that differentiate drug users from nonusers or describe clinically what makes up a "psychedelic personality."[55] Who are the drug users? What are they like? Let us look at the variables that have been discovered to be associated with drug-taking.

The 1969 "Masstown" study found that drug users differ from nonusers in some very important ways. With respect to academic performance, researchers found that less than two percent of those students whose grades are mostly As use drugs, while over three-quarters of those students whose grades are mostly Ds use drugs. The Great Neck (Long Island) High School study reveals a similar finding: less drug use among students with higher grades. These results differ sharply from the findings of Goldstein[56] and Walters et al.,[57] for whom grades are essentially uncorrelated with drug use. The situation may well be changing over time. In a 1970 article Richard C. Pillard[58] cites an unpublished survey that showed no substantial difference between high school age users and nonusers in terms of grades.

For the total "Masstown" sample the investigators found that over 80 percent of students have used alcohol. Drug users tend to be less moderate, however, in their consumption patterns. Eighty percent have been intoxicated, a large number of them frequently. Only 20 percent of the nonusers report ever having been intoxicated.

While the relationship between drug use and antisocial behavior has also been examined, the major findings (Masstown, Hogan in Pillard) remain unpublished. The "Masstown" study examined such behaviors as vandalism, shoplifting, stealing from institutions (such as school), stealing from individuals, fighting, being picked up by the police, and actually being booked on charges. The findings reveal that *all* of these acts are far more prevalent among the users than the nonusers. For example, 60 percent of the young people who use drugs have shoplifted while only 10 percent of the nonusers have. Students using drugs were found to be twice as likely as the others to be apprehended by the police for reasons other than drug use. The researchers also report that, contrary to a commonly held belief that drug users tend to be passive personalities, fighting behavior was positively associated with drug use. Over two-thirds of the users regularly engage in physical fights. Hogan's survey[59] reports similar results: that trouble with the law was more common among users than among nonusers.

Questioned about the quality of their lives and their feelings about school, drug users in "Masstown" are three times as likely as nonusers to say they are dissatisfied with their lives in general. Similar ratios show their dissatisfaction with their school situation. In *Voices from the Drug Culture* Pope makes the point that students have always complained about school. But he argues that young people today are complaining for different reasons. They feel their teachers are teaching nothing worth learning and that their education is "irrelevant to the business of living."[60]

Some information is available on family background variables. A consistent finding is that the parents' level of education and occupation does not disclose a difference between users and nonusers; nor does the fact of whether or not the mothers work.[f] What seems to matter most is family intactness, that is, whether or not both parents are present in the home. Studies[61] consistently show that children from families that are united have fewer problems with drugs.

The relationship between drug use and professional psychological help is not well understood. In "Masstown," inquiries about the student's history of professional help for emotional problems had an unexpected effect: many students wanted more help. There were no data on the proportion of students receiving help. For the most part, many young people in "Masstown" wanted an opportunity to talk over problems in groups or with an adult individually; about 40 percent of the *total* sample felt this would be beneficial.

Young people in general (whether they use drugs or not) often

---

[f]Found in the "Masstown" survey.

lack accurate information about the substances they do or do not ingest. Only about 25 percent in "Masstown" knew, for example, that serious physical damage could be caused by sniffing glue. There was considerable confusion about the effects of marijuana. About 50 percent of the students polled believed that marijuana was physically addicting. A similar proportion did not believe it could produce psychological dependence.

The picture we get, then, of the modal drug user in "Masstown" is that of a youngster who is having difficulty in school; who is generally unhappy with life; who engages in some form of antisocial behavior; and who probably would like understanding and help from his family and adults in his community. The evidence does not imply that *all* "Masstown" users have these characteristics. Failing to point this out is an error frequently made by professionals interested in understanding the drug problem, not only by the lay public. Recognition of the extraordinarily broad *spectrum* of drug users is essential if we are to meet them on their own grounds, and to provide psychological assistance and educational programs.

Brotman, Silverman, and Suffet[62] investigated correlates of drug use in terms of three social roles that every adolescent must fulfill —son or daughter, student, friend. They found that nonusers were likelier to conform to the stereotype of the teenager who fulfills these roles in an ideal way. Nonusers tended to be involved with their families and school, and their peer activities often centered on sports and TV. Users, on the other hand, were more concerned with broad societal issues, less with fulfilling the requirements of conventional roles. Their peer activities tended to be more cultural, aesthetic, and nonschool and nonhome related.

A 1972 study of college students by Walters et al.[63] reports no differences between users and nonusers in respect to grades, athletics, and school activities. Instead, they found that drug use was related to differences in self-concept, and differences in values and attitudes, as suggested by subjective alienation (self-reported feelings of alienation), visits to psychiatrists, fewer definite career plans, and greater sexual activity.

The most comprehensive studies of correlates of drug use in college are those of Blum and his associates. We will look only at the results of their most recent (1969) efforts.[64] A comparison of abstainers[g] with the complete sample indicates that abstainers tend

---

[g]They use no drugs, including alcohol and tobacco.

to be younger, poorer, more conservative, more religious, and more satisfied with their present and future prospects in life. From our point of view this analysis would have been far more revealing had abstention not included alcohol or tobacco use. We might then have obtained a clearer picture of the characteristics of users vs. nonusers of drugs.

The investigators adduced a large number of traits associated with extensive drug-taking. The most experienced users are: wealthier, older upperclassmen, irreligious, politically left-wing and active, oppose their parents on many issues, major in arts, humanities, or social sciences, undergo ideological shifts, are generally dissatisfied with school, and pessimistic about the future. The authors say they really cannot be sure about the dynamics underlying these trends. They speculate that exposure to drugs and pro-drug arguments may greatly influence a student's decision to use drugs. Thus, the correlates of age and year in school tend to make sense; the longer the student has been in school, the more he has been exposed to propaganda. The correlates also suggest that general dissatisfaction, low morale, and the alienation felt by many of these students serve as catalysts for the search for new experiences. A later study by Walters et al.[65] bears out the notion that a feeling of alienation is associated with drug use. Students who said they felt alienated tended to be users, whereas those who felt fairly close to traditional society and comfortable about their place in it tended not to use drugs.

Blum also found a consistent trend: all drug users tended to have more experience with other psychoactive agents (such as anesthesia). Furthermore, an examination of motives for drug-taking discloses that illicit users tend to make substantially exaggerated claims about what drug use accomplishes. For them drugs are broadly potent tools to reach a multitude of personal and interpersonal goals.[h]

A fascinating set of findings emerges from inquiries into parental medicating habits and students' recollections of "being sick" when they were young. Users of all drugs consistently reported the advantages of being sick as a child. The secondary gains, such as being able to avoid school, were many. Another small group of users remembered that during their childhood their parents showed little concern about their health. Consider the following:

[h]See earlier section on motives.

As to the gains from childhood illness, the speculations that emerge are tantalizing. Were these gains an introduction to passivity compatible with adult drug-induced states? Were the self-indulgences in staying away from school and responsibility comparable with dropping-out, taking incompletes, and enjoying pleasure-giving drugs? Were they early exposures to drugs which helped teach drug pleasures, now elaborated in adolescence? Were they periods of rest from excessive demands by ambitious parents or periods of attention from parents otherwise too busy to care? Were they, perhaps, early expressions of preoccupation with inner states—including symptoms—which foretold later investments in self-exploration through drugs? Are the data simply compatible with McGlothlin and Cohen's (1965) finding to the effect that drug-interested students enjoy regressive stages? Or is adult drug use simply a new way of gaining adult attention that was, in the earlier years, accompanied by being sick?[66]

Few studies have connected drug-taking to childhood illness and to a parent's and a child's responses to that illness.[i] A number of theorists[j] have proclaimed that we are a "pill-taking society." But the Blum study forces us to face the implications of taking pills. Pursuing his line of inquiry further, as the National Commission did, may help us to understand the etiology of the pill-taking phenomenon, and perhaps even to develop effective modes of intervention.

Thanks to these many studies and research reports, our knowledge about students who use drugs has developed significantly. So have the hypotheses that attempt to predict who will or will not take drugs. Yet, most of these theories were built on data furnished by older users—generally of college age, occasionally high school students. We still know remarkably little, psychologically speaking, about the youngest users and nonusers. How do they decide whether or not to use drugs? What determines continued use? What is their usage pattern? The answers are important; for in the 1960s, public attitudes changed enough that it could be said, "the tables have turned with a vengeance." Today in some communities, among older adolescents, nonusers are in the minority and may actually be made to feel "deviant" by virtue of abstinence. Drugs are increasingly accessible to younger and younger teenagers. How may they respond? We now turn to a study of several young teenagers.

---

[i]George Demos and John W. Shainline studied the propensity to take drugs without medical advice and found that individuals with a history of unsupervised drug use tend to be more likely to take hallucinogenics.

[j]See earlier sections.

Notes

1. Ernest Harms, ed., *Drug Addiction in Youth*, New York: Pergamon Press, 1965; and David Solomon, ed. *The Marihuana Papers*, New York: New American Library, 1966.

2. Ernest Harms, *Drug Addiction in Youth*, p. 20.

3. Sidney Cohen, *The Drug Dilemma*, New York: McGraw-Hill, 1969.

4. Richard Blum and Associates, *Society and Drugs*, San Francisco: Jossey-Bass Inc., 1969.

5. Ernest Harms, *Drug Addiction in Youth*.

6. Richard Blum and Associates, *Society and Drugs*.

7. Ibid.

8. David Solomon, ed., *The Marihuana Papers*.

9. Sidney Cohen, *The Drug Dilemma*.

10. Richard Blum and Associates, *Society and Drugs*.

11. Sidney Cohen, *The Drug Dilemma*.

12. Helen Nowlis, *Drugs on the College Campus*, New York: Doubleday-Anchor Books, 1969, p. 23.

13. Sidney Cohen, *The Drug Dilemma*, p. xi.

14. Richard Blum and Associates, *Students and Drugs*, San Francisco: Jossey-Bass Inc., 1969; George Demos and John W. Shainline, "Drug Use on the College Campus: A Pilot Study," unpublished; and Kenneth Eells, "Marihuana and LSD: A Survey of one College Campus," *Journal of Counseling Psychology* 15(5) (1968).

15. Samuel Pearlman, "Drug Use and Experience in an Urban College Population," *American Journal of Orthopsychiatry* 38(3) (1968).

16. Richard Blum and Associates, *Students and Drugs*; George Demos and John W. Shainline, "Drug Use on the College Campus;" and Kenneth Eells, "Marihuana and LSD."

17. George Demos and John W. Shainline, "Drug Use on the College Campus;" Kenneth Eells, "Marihuana and LSD;" and Samuel Pearlman, "Drug Use and Experience in an Urban College Population."

18. Samuel Pearlman, "Drug Use and Experience in an Urban College Population."

19. Kenneth Eells, "Marihuana and LSD."

20. Ernest Harms, *Drug Addiction in Youth*.

21. Richard Blum and Associates, *Students and Drugs*.

22. Ibid.

23. Donald B. Louria, *The Drug Scene*, New York: McGraw-Hill, 1968.

24. Richard Blum and Associates, *Students and Drugs*.

25. Boston Evening Globe, March 16, 1970.

26. Richard Blum and Associates, *Students and Drugs*, p. 362.

27. Donald B. Louria, *The Drug Scene*.

28. Erich Goode, ed., *Marijuana*, New York: Atherton Press, 1969.

29. Richard Blum and Associates, *Students and Drugs*.

30. Ibid., p. 342.

31. Ibid., p. 341.

32. Ibid., p. 341.

33. Herbert Blumer, "The World of Youthful Drug Use," Addiction Center Final Report, University of California at Berkeley, 1967.

34. Ibid., p. 59.

35. Richard Goldstein, *1 in 7: Drugs on Campus*, New York: Walker and Co., 1966.

36. Richard Blum and Associates, *Society and Drugs*.

37. Richard Goldstein, *1 in 7: Drugs on Campus*.

38. Harrison Pope, Jr., *Voices from the Drug Culture*, Cambridge, Mass.: The Sanctuary, 1971.

39. Richard Goldstein, *1 in 7: Drugs on Campus*, p. 21.

40. Ibid., p. 22.

41. Richard Blum and Associates, *Students and Drugs*.

42. Norman Zinberg, "Facts and Fancies about Drug Addiction," *Public Interest* 6 (1967).

43. Ibid., p. 86.

44. David Solomon, *The Marihuana Papers*.

45. Ibid., p. 79.

46. Donald B. Louria, *The Drug Scene*.

47. Sidney Cohen, *The Drug Dilemma*.

48. Donald B. Louria, *The Drug Scene*, p. 32.

49. Harrison Pope, Jr., *Voices from the Drug Culture*.

50. Ibid., p. 15.

51. In Richard C. DeBold and Russel Leaf, eds., *LSD, Man, and Society*, Wesleyan University Press, 1967.

52. David Solomon, *The Marihuana Papers*.

53. Richard Blum and Associates, *Students and Drugs*.

54. Quote from Goodman and Gilman, 1955, in Dana Farnsworth, "Drugs—Their Use and Abuse by College Students," in *Psychiatry, Education and the Young Adult*, Springfield, Illinois: Charles C. Thomas, 1966.

55. James H. Kleckner, "Personality Differences Between Psychedelic Drug Users and Non-Users," *Psychology* 5(2) (1968).

56. Richard Goldstein, *1 in 7: Drugs on Campus*.

57. Paul A. Walters, Jr., George W. Goethals, and Harrison G. Pope, Jr., "Drug Use and Life Style Among 500 College Undergraduates," *Archives of General Psychiatry* 26 (1972).

58. Richard C. Pillard, "Marihuana," *New England Journal of Medicine* 283(6) (August 1970).

59. Ibid.

60. Harrison Pope, Jr., *Voices from the Drug Culture*.

61. Massachusetts Drug Rehabilitation Survey 1969; Hogan in Richard C. Pillard, "Marihuana;" and Richard Blum and Associates, *Students and Drugs*.

62. In Erich Goode, ed., *Marijuana*.

63. Paul A. Walters, Jr. et al., "Drug Use and Life Style Among 500 College Undergraduates."

64. Richard Blum and Associates, *Students and Drugs*.

65. Paul A. Walters, Jr. et al., "Drug Use and Life Style Among 500 College Undergraduates."

66. Richard Blum and Associates, *Students and Drugs*, p. 97-98.

3

Gathering the Data

The Sample

Studies of drug use[a] would be greatly facilitated if three conditions could be fulfilled: if random samples of known users versus non-users could be drawn; if personal background data from each child's parents and school were readily available; and if anonymity could be guaranteed. But all three conditions pose barriers. Because of the illegality of drug-taking as well as the highly charged atmosphere surrounding any investigation of use, school systems are not good places to collect data, especially personal or psychological data. Moreover, protecting a subject's anonymity is difficult. Finally, few students tend to volunteer in such a public atmosphere; it is unlikely the ones who do represent any sort of random sample. There are other difficulties. For example, in their 1969 study of adolescents, Norman A. Sprinthall and Ralph L. Mosher[1] found their subjects unwilling to talk about highly personal matters with examiners whom they did not know. Thus I thought it advantageous to draw cases for study from a "referred" population. Research by medical doctors is frequently restricted to such a referred population, e.g., patients in hospitals, for similar reasons.

For the last few years I have worked as a consulting psychologist with a small group of colleagues. We offer consulting services to individuals and organizations. Primary among these services are educational and vocational guidance and diagnostic evaluations. Young people and their parents ask us about school placement, their motivational and achievement difficulties, and bring up issues related to ability, behavior, and personality. Referrals for diagnostic consultations come from diverse sources—pediatricians, psychotherapists, and public and private school personnel. A very large part of our client population, therefore, consists of youngsters of school-age.

---

[a]"Drugs" will mean primarily marijuana. However, subjects have not been excluded if they have used other more potent drugs, such as LSD, speed, mescaline, etc., in addition to marijuana.

Table 3-1
The Student Sample[a]

	Nonusers			Users				
	Male	Male	Male	Female	Female	Male	Female	Male
Age	14	14	14	14	15	13	15	14
Grade when seen by me	9	8	8	9	9	7	9	8

[a]These were the subjects selected from my consulting practice.

I selected the cases for this study from our files, according to the following criteria: (1) The evaluation had been done by me. (2) The student was attending junior high school (grade 7, 8, 9) at the time he was seen in our office. (3) The interview material contained a yes or no answer to the question, "Have you ever used any drugs?"

Initially, 10 students were identified who met these requirements. Five said they had used marijuana—though three of them said only once. Five had never used any illegal drug. I sent a letter to each child's parents asking their permission for his or her participation. Promising anonymity, I also requested permission to use the interviews and test data.

The initial 10 letters brought nine favorable replies—from five users and four nonusers. Unfortunately, scheduling problems allied to the required series of in-depth interviews precluded my seeing all nine. Also, two of the initial nonusers became users in the interim, and so, a second effort to obtain nonusers was made. I scheduled as many new junior high school-age clients as possible. The end result was five users and three nonusers; Table 3-1 describes the sample.

There is, clearly, no reasonable way to argue that these young people represent any sort of random sample of all junior high school-age students in America. Each one was part of a special subgroup of the population—the group that consults a psychologist for some sort of educational or psychological problem. In this respect they differ from the norm. The major implication of this limitation, together with the small sample size, is that we must be extremely cautious in generalizing about any large junior high school population on the basis of these eight children. The great value of studying them closely is that we can develop detailed case histories for a few individuals. Richard Goldstein, Harrison Pope, Richard

Blum, and others have carried out some in-depth studies with adults and college students. But for high school and junior high school students, similar case studies are virtually nonexistent. We can learn a great deal from a few children. This has been a "modus operandi" for psychologists going back to Freud.

Data Collection Procedures

I saw each student for approximately five interviews lasting one to three hours each. The interviews combined structured and open-ended questions. At the beginning of the series of interviews each student was told that, as a volunteer, he was free to refuse to answer any question.

The major categories of inquiry were based chiefly on the significant findings of Blum[2] and others for college students, and the results of the "Masstown" survey of students in public and parochial schools, grades 7 to 12. Several categories were added or deleted in consideration of the age (appropriateness) of these young students.

Here, in outline form, are the areas covered in the series of interviews (a more detailed guide to the interview appears in Appendix A).

1. *How person started using marijuana (other drugs)*. In order to understand the enormous rise in drug use, we should know something about the circumstances that led to the adolescent's initiation to the drug scene. Here we would want to know:
   a) When did first use occur?
   b) Where?
   c) With whom, if anyone?
   d) How the drug was obtained—bought, given?
   e) Nature of the decision-making process—spur of the moment, something mulled over for a long time, on a dare, etc.?
   f) Major reason for first use, if any?
2. *Description of first drug experience*. Other investigators repeatedly stress that the pleasurable aspects of marijuana use are learned. Therefore, the first experience may not be particularly satisfying. It would then be useful to know:
   a) How the drug made the person feel.

b) Compare (a) with what he or she expected.

c) What the affective state was resulting from the first try.

d) Person's attitude toward trying it again.

3. *Pattern of use after first experience.* The college student studies,[3] (reviewed in Chapter 2) differentiated users on the basis of frequency of use: they ranged from "experimenters" to "heads." I was interested to see whether such categorizations were possible or reasonable with much younger users. This field of inquiry included questions about:

a) More information on what the drug accomplishes for the user.

b) If the first-time effect was not good, what motivated continuation.

c) Circumstances in which use occurs.

d) The affect associated with an act the person knows is illegal and frowned upon by society.

e) Attitude towards one's own drug use and plans for the future—whether or not student plans to continue using drugs or stop. Why? What would make him stop?

f) What he feels his psychological needs are, if any, for using drugs, or if it is just a way to have fun.

4. *Feelings about achievement.* Earlier studies do not examine the relationship between the need for achievement and drug use. Laymen have frequently suggested that achievement motivation and drug use are inversely related: that drug use is linked to passivity; and, finally, that drug use is a form of rebellion against achievement-oriented values. I wanted, wherever possible, to examine a person's attitudes toward achievement before, during, and after (if he had quit) the period of drug use. I thought it also would be interesting to get this information from the parents concerned as well as from their children. Some evidence about each subject's feeling of satisfaction regarding school was sought as well.

5. *Academic performance.* Almost every report on college students[4] found little or no relationship between grades and frequency of drug use. In sharp contrast, the "Masstown" study, indicated that a higher proportion of D students than A students used drugs. Because of my small sample I could not hope to test formally any hypotheses about relationships be-

tween drug use and academic performance. However, I wanted to look at the pattern of grades before and after the onset of drug-taking in this group.

6. *Relationship between drug use and need for friends.* Psychological theory underscores the importance of the peer group in early adolescence. Sidney Cohen[5] and Donald B. Louria[6] both feel that a major motivation for use lies within the peer group. At a time of questioning the omniscience of parents a child generally moves toward his peers; he is strongly influenced by their standards and has a strong need to be accepted. Peer pressure together with the desire for acceptance by a peer group seemed to me potentially major factors in both initial and continued drug use. Here I wanted data on:

a) When the student uses drugs: alone or with others? With what kind of group?

b) Do good friends use drugs?

c) Was initial use encouraged by someone the young person knows?

d) What pattern of friendship existed before and after use?

e) Did use help to establish more friendships?

7. *Relationship to older sibling use.* This area seemed worth exploring. In addition to peer influence, another influential factor might be a person's desire to identify with his older sibling.

8. *Medication orientation of the family.* One of Richard Blum's[7] most provocative findings about college students was a strong association between parental medicating habits and a child's drug use. I was interested to see whether or not this was true also for younger adolescents.

9. *Relationship between student and parents.* Since many people believe that drug use is a form of adolescent rebellion or "acting out" against parental authority and values, I wanted to examine closely each parent-child relationship. Blum[8] concluded that basic value disagreements were associated with drug use; I pursued this suggestion. I also inquired:

a) How close is the relationship? Do parents ever say "I love you" or praise the student?

b) Does the student feel his parents are "with" him or "against" him? Would they stand behind him?

c) Have they discussed the issue of drug use? What reasons, if any, do the parents give to discourage drug use? What did they (or would they) do if they discovered their child was using drugs?

10. *Experience with cigarettes and alcohol.*

11. *Ideas and attitudes toward intervention.* Here I wanted to learn if young teenagers felt anything should be done to help them and their peers to stay away from drugs; their attitude toward the legalization of drugs; and their experience, if any, with drug education programs.

The nonusers were queried in many of these areas, and in great detail, about their reasons for not taking drugs. I proposed several hypothetical situations in order to determine how strongly they felt about not using drugs.

In addition to the interview material, the following data, collected during the previous year, were available in my file on each student: a history-taking interview with parents, an interview with the child, an intelligence test (Wechsler or Binet), achievement tests in reading and mathematics (Cooperative Reading Test and mathematics section from the Sequential Tests of Educational Progress) and projective tests (Rotter Incomplete Sentence Blank, Visual Impressions Test, Thematic Apperception Test, Rorschach Inkblot Test).

All the interviews were conducted throughout 1971. Both subjects and parents were cooperative and enthusiastic about participating in the study. As the previous chapter indicates, it is very difficult to get young people to look at their behavior and try to explain it. Often the retrospective look is painful, embarrassing, or distorted in order to make sense of it. Yet in this study no student ever refused to answer any question that was asked of him. It is my strong impression that such a cooperative and willing spirit is simply a function of a strong preexisting relationship. I was rather surprised that none of the students seemed concerned about anonymity or confidentiality. They asked no questions about who would have access to the data.

Notes

1. Norman A. Sprinthall and Ralph L. Mosher, *Studies of Adolescents in Secondary School*, Cambridge, Mass: Center for Research and Development on Educational Differences, 1969.

2. Richard Blum and Associates, *Students and Drugs*, San Francisco: Jossey-Bass, Inc. 1969.

3. Richard Goldstein, *1 in 7: Drugs on Campus*, New York: Walker & Co., 1966; Donald B. Louria, *The Drug Scene*, New York: McGraw-Hill, 1968.

4. Richard Blum and Associates, *Students and Drugs*; Paul A. Walters, Jr. et al., "Drug Use and Life Style Among 500 College Undergraduates," *Archives of General Psychiatry* 26 (1972).

5. Sidney Cohen "The Cyclic Psychedelics," *American Journal of Psychiatry* 125 (1968).

6. Donald B. Louria, *The Drug Scene*.

7. Richard Blum and Associates, *Students and Drugs*.

8. Ibid.

4

The Children Speak

Finally we meet the kids.[a] Five are drug users: Ellen, Randi, Paul, Barbara, and Tom. Three are nonusers: Kevin, Mark, and Lenny. Here is a brief picture of each so that you can get to know them and how they happened to get involved (or did not) with drugs.

Users

Ellen

I first met Ellen when she was in the ninth grade at a prestigious country day school. She had been sent to see me by the headmaster because he could not understand why she was not doing better in her classes. Ellen presented herself as a reticent youngster. She answered my questions in almost inaudible tones. She fidgeted with her fingers in her lap and avoided my gaze. After discussing her school history, which included repeating eighth grade, Ellen said that she was working hard, but found it impossible to write papers in English or history—"I can't get started or end the paper." Her parents feel that Ellen is more motivated by matters social than academic, and that she does not associate learning with pleasure. "Her papers are so immature," said Mr. T., "that you could weep. Establishing her social position takes precedence."

Ellen is the fourth child in a family of six. She has three sisters, two older and one younger, and two brothers, one older, one younger. Her father is a businessman; her mother is at home. Mr. and Mrs. T. appeared to be quite concerned about Ellen, not only in connection with her school work, but also with their poor rapport. "We don't feel we communicate well—we're often on different wavelengths. I know she's distressed, but I don't know why."

Outside of school, Ellen said, she enjoys spending her time skiing, sailing, and playing tennis, which she does with more compe-

---

[a]The students' names have been changed to protect their identities.

tence than her schoolwork. Also, she enjoys spending time with several close friends and with her boyfriend. In discussing Ellen's interpersonal relationships, Mr. and Mrs. T. said that she gets along well with others, but "she is so easily led" and "her fault is niceness—she's too nice."

At the time we first met, Ellen had used marijuana a few times. She said she had never gotten stoned. Also, she was not interested in trying any other drugs—"They scare me."

About a year later, as I began this book, the T's got in touch with me for help in finding another school for Ellen. She had been kicked out of school for dealing in marijuana.

When I saw Ellen at this later time, she looked older, somewhat "tougher." Her posture and speech conveyed a sense of confidence which had not been apparent in our early meetings. The interview began spontaneously with a discussion of her new school and of how she was caught selling marijuana. She said that her parents were "pretty good" about her expulsion.

I'd gotten suspended once for drugs and been doing them all summer. I thought they didn't care cuz there were other family worries. I tried mescaline and acid. I decided to get screwed up so they'd worry about me.

Ellen's drug experience began in grade eight with marijuana. During the summer following ninth grade, she was smoking every day. That year she had taken LSD more than 10 times, as well as speed, sleeping pills, mescaline, and cocaine. Drugs were readily available in her home town. At present, Ellen had "stopped all chemicals" largely because of Jim, a 20-year-old friend, who had gone straight and convinced Ellen to do the same. "He got sick of it . . . did it for pleasure . . . cuz it's the same over and over, in the same atmosphere with the same people, music, etc. . . . ." "Anyway," added Ellen, "I've gotten out of being shy and so I don't need to any more."

Ellen's first three experiences with marijuana were not very memorable; she did not get high.[1] The fourth time occurred when Ellen and a friend were skiing. "Sitting there it hit me—I tried to fight it because I couldn't realize I was doing it. I kept saying 'Am I high?'"

Ellen's first experiences were not really planned. She had been thinking about trying marijuana, but it was not until her brother offered her some that she actually decided to go ahead with it.

Mainly, Ellen said, she wanted to sample marijuana because she did not believe what people said about feeling completely different. Being stoned made her forget her depression. She expected to hallucinate and "be out of my mind and out of control. . . . It was much more pleasant than that."

After these first few experiences, during which she felt completely relaxed, Ellen could only think, "Quick—let's go get more." But it was several months before she smoked again. Drugs were not so easily available.

Clearly, Ellen was consciously or unconsciously looking for a way to get some attention from her parents. In a family of six children a quiet child who does not "make waves" can go unnoticed. That is how Ellen felt. In addition, although she was yearning for closeness with others, she saw herself as shy and incompetent. She was, at the outset, depressed and lonely.

Ellen continued doing marijuana mostly because she enjoyed it. She tried acid and mescaline to forget her depression and "downs" to relax and help her sleep. For Ellen, drugs were taken as a good time on one level, but as a facilitator on another. "I used to be really shy; now I'm not. I used to embarrass easily; now I don't. Speed made me talk; I had a thing about talking to people—no self-confidence and I expected to be cut down for talking. Someone suggested speed was a way to help with talking. Now I say whatever is on my mind. At first I'd think about what I was saying; then I didn't. People accept you if they're gonna."

In response to, "Is life more fun with drugs?" Ellen said, "No. I used to think that. If you want, you can have a natural high all your life, by being yourself—they'll like you or not."

Ellen did her drugs alone and with others, at home, on the beach, walking through town. Most of her friends are older (16-20) and have used them. Ellen reported always wishing she had more friends; in the past summer she gained entrée to a crowd she wanted to join. "They'd all gone to public school. I'd always been in private school. Soon they forgot about it." At one point she smoked every day for three to four months; at another, "I tripped or did something else as often as possible—maybe three times a week." She reported that working hard in school comes more naturally since doing drugs, and that her grades had risen a lot. "In fact, working was just more enjoyable."

Doing something illegal does not bother Ellen much; however, the fact that drugs are frowned on has recently begun to bother her. She says she thinks of her parents and feels guilty. Her future plans include grass, but no chemicals. Jim and her father were instrumental in Ellen's discontinuation of more potent drugs. Her parents are aware of the extent of her drug experience. Mr. T. reportedly reacted with no shock or anger. Mrs. T. was concerned about "what my friends will think."

Ellen was glad to talk about her experiences. She ended our series of interviews by remarking, "It's mostly in the past . . . nothing I'm especially proud of but it was an important experience and it's good to talk about it."

Randi

Mrs. B. brought 14-year-old Randi to see me during her eighth grade year in school because she wanted help in finding a private school for her. She believed in an education that combined the merits of public and private schools. Also, she was concerned about her daughter's declining marks (since fourth grade) and about the defiant group Randi was in. The girl was not interested in going to private school, in talking with me, or in taking any tests. Her responses were perfunctory; she appeared to be bored but dutiful.

Mrs. B. left her first husband (Randi's father) before Randi was born, lived alone for many years, and then remarried. Her second marriage was not successful either: she has been separated for almost five years. Mrs. B. never worked until several years ago—"when I had to"; she does clerical work. Randi, the younger of two children, has a lot of contact with her stepfather who lives nearby, but none with her real father.

Randi describes herself as an average student, "not too good." She does not like school, academically speaking, but likes the social side of things. Besides riding and gymnastics, in which she is an active participant, Randi mainly enjoys just being with friends—"just being together . . . we do lots of things . . . do what we want." Mrs. B. reported that Randi's friends are the only strain in their relationship. She describes them as being too concerned about money, having negative attitudes: "they think nothing of running away." When I asked, "Is Randi easily led—is that what worries you?" Mrs. B. replied, "She likes to be liked . . . that means going along . . . there's one girl with whom she gets into trouble.'' Like most adolescents, Randi, according to her mother, seeks her identity by identifying with prevailing group norms and patterns. In my view, Randi follows along rather than leads: she really does not see herself as having much "going for her." It is better to "go along" rather than to be left out.

To my surprise, Randi agreed to participate in this study. She was smiling, friendly, and more talkative than she had been when we first met. At that earlier time she said she had tried pot once.

Randi's drug experience began at the start of her ninth grade year. She said she had been thinking about trying marijuana over the whole summer. "I never thought it was anything so bad. I didn't know if I wanted to or should." Randi finally decided that she wanted to find out what everyone was talking about. So with two friends her age, one of whom had purchased the marijuana, Randi smoked pot for the first time in a local park. She reported being "surprised it did anything to me cuz I didn't expect anything. I felt really happy and giggly . . . Everything looked so good . . . I was in a really good mood . . . Everything looked better because I felt better.'' She liked her first experience so much—"Why not do it again?''

Randi continued smoking pot occasionally (10-12 times) throughout her last year in junior high. She did it because she liked the good feeling it gave her. Each experience was "basically the same . . . I could usually tell what would happen each time and I could control it.'' Using marijuana made life somewhat more exciting for Randi. "I'm not just the same all the time." She never smoked alone; she was always with the same two friends—her boyfriend and a girl. Smoking pot usually occurred at the park, in someone's house (never her own), or in a car.

Randi has no desire to take other more potent drugs. She is now using marijuana every week, usually on the weekends. She ended our conversation by saying she is scared about "getting busted," but that is not worrisome enough to make her stop. "If I was caught by the police or my mother, I'd just get more cautious. Nothing would stop me altogether. My mother knows—just not how often.''

In many ways Randi is a typical suburban middle-class teenager. She is an average student and, except for sports, has no exceptional talents. Being "with the kids" is her major spare time activity. I hear that phrase so often—"being with the kids." If I ask what they do together the usual answer is "just hang around . . . talk." The need to be with people is intense for young teenagers like Randi. They are on the threshhold of establishing close relationships for the first time. But the relationships first tend to center around a group. Thus the group norms and attitudes become critical in defining acceptable behavior and values.

Paul

When Mr. and Mrs. P. brought 13-year-old Paul to see me they were coming out of a state of shock. Paul had just completed seventh grade at a private day school. Shortly before the end of the year the family had been informed that, although Paul passed all of his courses, he would not be allowed to return in September. They wanted help in finding a school for Paul.

"It's all politics," said Mr. P. "Their objection to Paul was political—they think our home is too liberal—we discuss all subjects, Vietnam, Abbie Hoffman, and marijuana. They thought Paul knew too much for his age. We were stunned. They said Paul had been seen in 'the wrong places.'" I asked what places he meant. He replied with a wry smile, "Harvard Square."

Paul, an extremely articulate young man, told me that he had enjoyed School X at first. He thought the sports and electives were great. He soon discovered that it was a pretty conservative place. A drug addict came to school to talk, "but sixth and seventh graders weren't even allowed to go!" In other words, "they don't like opposition to what they're doing. . . ." Paul had disagreed vocally with rules about dress and hair. "The teachers voted, I think, and decided that I was a bad influence." Like many young people, Paul was intensely interested in "now" things—movies, music, drugs. He read voraciously. In between tests and during his lunch break he was deeply engrossed in *A Child's Garden of Grass*. He wanted to talk about his reading and did so with considerable thoughtfulness and sensitivity.

Paul's experience at School X made him cautious about trusting people, including me. "He had trusted his teachers with his openness about many topics," commented Mrs. P., "but they betrayed him." Paul wrote an essay arguing for the legalization of marijuana, which he considered a major negative part of the dossier leading to his expulsion.

Paul is the oldest of two P. children. His father is a prominent businessman; his mother is at home. Mr. and Mrs. P. were obviously concerned about what they felt was the unjust way Paul had been treated. They remarked that Paul is a "great talker—very articulate and persuasive," and that, while they believe in open discussion of issues, arguments with Paul were frequent. In fact, they said, they are liberal "idea-wise," but not about Paul's behavior. "We're pretty rigid about his being home at night."

In and out of school, Paul was a busy young man. His parents encouraged activities. His interests and pursuits were wide-ranging, from playing the guitar with great competence, to wrestling, to ceramics. In addition, he loved to read. Most of his activities were solitary and rather intellectual for a 13-year-old. Paul said he had had a lot of friends in public school, but did not like those at private school much. It was hard to see his old friends because his school schedule was quite different from theirs. So, said Paul, "I'm lonely."

During this initial interview Paul said he had never done any drugs, except marijuana once: He was planning to take it again, but his parents found the marijuana in his room. He promised his father that he would not do it again—"and I have to keep it." He said he did not have any interest in trying other drugs, although the pressures at school were intense. My first interview notes include my qualification—"I'm not sure I really believe him."

Paul was an enthusiastic participant. He loved to talk about current issues and about himself. He was curious about how his responses compared with those of the others. Also, he volunteered to bring several interested friends as subjects, if I needed them.

His first experience with marijuana occurred during the summer preceding our meeting. He was then 12. Paul explained, "I'd been reading about it . . . was fascinated by it . . . by the accounts I read of Dumas and others . . . the reason I wouldn't do it was cuz I was worried there was heroin in it. When my friend corrected that, then I felt o.k. about it. Also, I was afraid of losing control . . . but I saw him stoned and knew I didn't have to worry." With his 14-year-old friend, who provided the marijuana, Paul had his first marijuana experience at camp.

"What did it do for you, Paul?" I asked. "It blew my mind. We were in a field with high reeds, watching the birds and insects . . . fabulous. . . . It was better than I expected—better than any LSD trip. I felt totally relaxed—the body rushes were overwhelming. The experience was so positive, I could hardly wait to smoke again." But "there was nowhere to get it" and so the next time was some six months later.

"I enjoyed it so much—continuing was just a natural course." Since fall 1970, Paul has been smoking pot daily. At about the same time he began using marijuana regularly, Paul got curious about other drugs. He tried LSD several times. "The first two times were best—LSD is more visual than marijuana. . . . I became very thoughtful and would do work (writing theories) while tripping." Paul switched from LSD to mescaline because of the reports that LSD causes brain tissue damage. He has used mescaline more than 30 times, mainly at concerts. "The visual and auditory effects are great . . . I'm in complete control." During the same year (1970-71) Paul used speed occasionally, sniffed cocaine once, and used psilocybin more than 30 times. "So some days I just smoke pot and some days I do something else. You know, hash and wine go great."

"Most of my friends are preoccupied with drugs. It's the main thing in their lives." So it is with Paul. He sells ("I don't push") marijuana to friends who want to buy. He has, what he considers, reliable contacts in town. About half the time Paul does drugs with friends. The rest of the time he smokes alone. "We do it in other people's houses. My friends are allowed to smoke pot. Their parents don't care—they don't like it, but they don't bother the kids about it. I like rolling a beautiful joint and smoking it down. That's perfect!"

While using drugs consumed much of his time and energy, Paul was still busy with his music and reading. His new school was "great" and he was doing well, though still less well than he could. He said he had begun to realize the importance of study and knowledge. "That's a coincidence. I don't think drugs have anything to do with that insight."

For Paul pleasure was the only conscious reason for doing drugs. However, as he describes his experiences, Paul sounds more like a college-age user. Drugs enhance his creativity and his enjoyment of artistic activities. Also, his comment about "rolling a beautiful joint" suggests a pleasure in the ritual of drug use which is a major factor for many of the older users.

At the time of the first interview for this book, Paul had given up all drugs except marijuana and hashish. He was in the process of completing a deal to get a lot of marijuana. "Then I won't have to buy or deal any more though I don't know how long it will last me."

Paul likes to be straight too. That is part of being in control. He spent the summer of 1970 straight. "There was no wanting. I could leave it."

Nothing would make Paul stop using drugs. He is very careful not to get caught, especially since "my parents are very suspicious. I'm always very polite. I don't want to give them cause to suspect. If I listen to Jimmy Hendrix, they check my eyes." According to Paul, his parents have no idea of the extent of his drug involvement. While they used to be able to discuss things, that was no longer the case. "It was too much of a hassle. They were always talking about how 'it's just not necessary.'"

In contrast to Ellen and Randi, a good part of Paul's life was involved in acquiring and using drugs. He had developed a way to preserve his image (for his parents) as a "talker" rather than a "doer." In fact, in Richard Goldstein's[2] terms, Paul was near the "head" end of the continuum.

Tom

Fourteen-year-old Tom had just finished repeating the eighth grade at one of the most prestigious boarding schools in America when I first saw him. He had started out well, but spring brought a total academic collapse. The school wanted to know whether or not to keep him, and Tom said, "I don't know if I'm good for the school or if that school's good for me."

Choosing a prep school had been a great struggle. Tom's parents had been divorced since he was eight. Both had remarried. Everyone (mother, father, stepfather) wanted his say as to where Tom would go to school. His father wanted him at one place, his mother said, "no—too near father." And his stepfather wanted him to attend his alma mater. Tom ended up at his stepfather's school. No one asked him where *he* would like to be.

Tom resented repeating that year. It was boring, and he had trouble concentrating on his work: there was a lot of noise in the dorms. Furthermore, other people "got on my nerves." Tom was quickly chosen as the dorm scapegoat.

Life in the O. household was chaotic for Tom—it was filled with children. Tom did not refer to it as "home," but as "the house where I'm staying." The children included his younger sister, three younger stepbrothers, and a half brother. There were also two older stepbrothers and one older stepsister who were not living at home. His father and stepmother dwelled, with no children, in a neighboring state. His father was a writer, liberal and permissive. Mr. O, his stepfather, was in business. He was conservative, both politically and concerning how Tom should conduct himself. Mr. O. mentioned that Tom's academic demise yielded "a strong letter from me telling him it was time to shape up." In addition to his work, Mr. O., an ex-alcoholic, spent every night at Alcoholics Anonymous. He had been involved with that organization for more than a decade. Mrs. O. was busy with the household most of the time.

Most of Tom's spare moments seemed to be spent in trying to find some sort of peace. Home was chaotic not only because there were so many people around all the time but also because the interrelationships were so complex. Tom desperately wanted to get away from the tumult. He did not like team sports much, though his school pressed students hard to participate. For fun he liked to read, sail, swim, listen to music, and take pictures. Tom was pretty isolated at school. He wanted friends but did not make them easily. His stepfather commented, "He seems to spend an abnormal amount of time by himself, reading . . . no sports or physical activity." He was an easy target for the bullies and scapegoaters because he was somewhat weak looking and his sexual development had not been totally normal.

Unlike Ellen, Randi, and Paul, Tom had some problems in his early development: bedwetting, soiling, sleep disturbances. And while Randi's family was not intact, either, Tom's situation was different. He had two fathers who wanted to be "father" and have a say in his upbringing. In fact, Tom was the only boy in school to have two sets of warring parents arrive for Parents' Weekend. Mrs. O. was very concerned about Tom and decided at our first meeting that his problems were obviously psychological.

During the first interview Tom said that he had almost tried marijuana but had not. "I was never hot to." Mrs. O. had discussed drug use with Tom in connection with her husband's past drinking problem. Mr. O. said that Tom was pretty uninformed about drugs.

Tom's first drug experience occurred about a year later. He was at a friend's house with several boys his age, one of whom had some marijuana. "My friend asked and I said yes . . . kind of spur of the moment decision. My friends were doing it . . . I saw no reason not to."

Like many naive marijuana smokers, Tom's first try produced nothing. He said he did not think anything would happen. "I didn't think it was the real stuff. I thought I'd been gypped." He was eager to try again.

At about the same time he tried mescaline. A lot of people had told him it was fun and he had also read about it. "It wasn't like what I expected . . . sudden insight into things. It made me feel pleasant. It was something like I thought, only more subtle."

Since that time Tom has been smoking pot about once a week, more in the summer because it is more readily available then. "I wouldn't go looking for it." He reports that marijuana makes him enjoy things (listening to music, reading, photography, walking) a little more. "It doesn't always give me insight, but I feel good." This is his main reason for continuing. Also, "A lot of other people are doing it—my friends and others."

It was quite clear from talking with Tom that peer acceptance was instrumental in his use of drugs. He had gone from being a totally isolated boy last year, to joining the crowd to which he wanted to belong. And when he was alone, he enjoyed his solitary activities more.

Tom gave up mescaline after about six tabs because of one bad experience. He had been hitchhiking "under the influence" and was picked up by the police. He was so terrified that they would know that the "trip" turned into a nightmare. He says that he plans to continue marijuana use "as is," but is not interested in trying any other substances. "Basically, I'm just having fun. If I got arrested or found out it was dangerous, you know, addictive, or if it gave me a disease or if it was like LSD and you could go crazy, then I'd stop."

His school work has deteriorated somewhat. "I don't know if it's because of drugs or not. I don't think so. The main thing is drugs take up time, but I don't do homework in my spare time anyway. At least marijuana eases the frustrations I feel about my bad grades a little bit. They're still there though."

Tom has discussed drug use abstractly with his parents. The O.'s "really don't like it." His father is "more open-minded about it." Tom thinks his father has "a pretty good idea what I do—mainly from my attitude." He is sure the O.'s know nothing about his use.

At the close of our interview Tom remarked spontaneously, "You know it's really hard to pinpoint reasons . . . it has a lot to do with the mood I'm in. If I'm depressed it makes me more depressed. Marijuana heightens the mood I'm in. That's probably why I like it so much."

It seems to me, however, that the rationale is more complicated than Tom suggests. Note that while he has achieved some measure of peer acceptance, he is still quite isolated interpersonally. His spare time activities are solitary ones. But if marijuana is part of the scene, Tom is able to be alone with himself—to withstand the isolation—and even to derive some pleasure during it. Drugs help him achieve a kind of personal privacy which many adolescents crave. Many seem to need to keep unpleasant reality from intruding. They want their flights into fantasy, according to Anna Freud. And so it is with Tom. Marijuana helps him to live in both his real and fantasy worlds.

Barbara

Barbara decided not to return to school. It was not coed; she was sick of boarding (she had been there three years); and besides, she had been in so much trouble there that her reputation was a shambles. What she really wanted to do was go to the local high school. Mr. and Mrs. P. were puzzled. Barbara had said before she wanted to go away—so they agreed. Now she said she did not want that anymore. Yet she was clearly unsure: "Maybe I'll board if it's a really free school." Mrs. P. worried that the local high school would overwhelm Barbara—"After all this is her ninth year in private school."

Barbara is the youngest of three children by Mrs. P.'s first marriage. Barbara's father died when she was eight years old, and Mrs. P. is now remarried. Her husband, a very successful businessman, has two children by a previous marriage—a girl about Barbara's age and an older son.

Barbara felt her parents did not understand her very well, especially her mother. "She's blind about things having to do with what younger people do. I talk to her, but I can't talk about a lot of stuff with her—she wouldn't approve or understand." Mrs. P. was obviously frantic about Barbara; she described herself as "an uptight mother . . . I'm worried about the future for her. I want things for her—to be healthy, happy, and not to take drugs."

Once again, Barbara's developmental history, like Tom's, includes some problems: willful and stubborn behavior as an infant, persistent behavior problems in school. She was a "devil" even in kindergarten, reported Mrs. P. Her teachers found her difficult to handle—she wouldn't listen. She was defiant and daring. "She'll do anything!" said Mrs. P.

Barbara's drug experiences began when she had just started seventh grade. She and a friend each drank two bottles of cough syrup because they wanted to get high. Nothing happened, though: "I just got a headache." Very soon after that Barbara, home from school for the weekend, went to a party with a friend. A boy offered her some marijuana and she smoked it. "It was a very spur-of-the-moment decision. I didn't think about it. I just wanted to do it." She guessed that it was treated with something—"maybe MDA, cuz I hallucinated. I liked the feeling. When we were in the car coming home I remember seeing purple elephants coming out of a house." When I asked her how she felt about using it again, Barbara replied, "Wow—gotta get some."

The main reason Barabara continued to smoke pot was simple: she enjoyed it. Soon after, however, she began to experiment with other drugs. During the two-year period (ages 13-15), between grades seven and nine, Barbara used mescaline, speed, "downs," psilocybin, hash, opium, MDA, and LSD (more than 100 times). Drugs were readily available at her new school. "The day students bring them in; kids bring stuff back from weekends and it even gets sent through the mail."

"Why did you do all of those?" I asked. "Because I was very unhappy with my life. I was unhappy about where I was at school, about my friends, about home, and my parents. Life was a hassle . . . I really did it to seek happiness. All it got me was worse." For a time Barbara felt that even the bad trips were better than the real world. Her capacity to be alone, like that of most young teenagers today, to withstand even minor frustration, is minimal. Mostly she used drugs with a few people or by herself; large crowds made her feel "scared and crammed in."

Barbara reported that she stopped doing drugs at the start of her sophomore year. "Sure, I smoke pot, but I don't consider that a drug." She said that she stopped because "They messed me up. I had no head. I couldn't think at all. People only talked to me about drugs. They thought I only *knew* about drugs."

Her parents now know about her drug history, because she told them. "My mother still doesn't believe it. She denies it. She doesn't want to believe that her little girl is doing it." In contrast to the other drug users in this study, Barbara's use has gotten her into serious trouble. "I was busted in seventh grade at X, but my mother didn't tell my father. Then I got busted smoking in some park by the police. I got a six months' continuation with no finding. Then I got busted at school this year before I quit . . . There have been times when I've been pretty bratty, but my parents have always hung in. I never thought they shouldn't. I guess they helped me cuz I belong to them."

Barbara still has not quit using drug substances as an aid to living. She had been drinking every day for many months at the time we met. She was embarrassed when asked and did not want to say how much alcohol she was consuming, admitting "I drink to get drunk . . . cuz I enjoy it." Barbara reported that she was smoking marijuana less—"cuz I like drinking better . . . It brings out my whole inner self to everyone . . . [I] can really speak freely. I could do this with speed, say what I wanted to. That's important so people will know who you are. Otherwise, they're not knowing who you really are."

While Barbara's earlier friendships revolved primarily around drugs, now a great deal of her time with others is spent drinking. She is not really part of a crowd and says she has grown away from many old "druggie" friends. Besides drinking, Barbara says that she is "really into school now. Before drugs and during I wasn't. I don't know if that was caused by drugs. I got a few Fs when I was doing acid heavy. I used to get Cs and Ds; now I'm getting Bs."

As Barbara sees it, life is clearly better now than before. She says she now feels more in touch with her "real self." When I saw her last, she was again without a school for September (11th grade). She had been "busted out" for drinking. And family relationships were worse than ever. My impression was that Barbara was "talking a good line" and that deep down she was as unhappy as ever. But she did not want to face that.

Nonusers

Kevin

Kevin was 14 years old when I first saw him. He had come to see me for help in deciding whether or not to go to private school. He was then midway through his freshman year at a large suburban high school. Disappointed there, he said he preferred his junior high school, and wished that ninth grade could still be at his old school—"Most junior high schools go 7 to 9, don't they? There I looked forward to going each day."

School had always been a struggle for Kevin, reported his parents. "He read early and with alacrity, but had trouble completing written assignments. He was always young for his grade. He was so bright early on." The W.'s thought that the junior high had good teachers, or at least that Mr. W.'s being on the school committee helped. Both parents agreed that he would do better in a smaller school.

Like both his parents, Kevin was an only child. Mr. W. was a technical consultant, who worked long hours and spent about a third of his time traveling. Mrs. W. was basically a housewife, though she pursued a number of outside activities.

In our first meeting, Kevin was articulate but guarded in response to my questions. He gave brief, factual answers but offered no spontaneous comments. He did not know whether or not he wanted to go to boarding school. "I'd like to meet different people, but it worries me—you know, starting over in a new place." Further questioning revealed that Kevin had few friends; he had always had just a few. "There aren't too many nearby cuz where we live is like an island; it's separated from the main part of town. Don't know many kids . . . so I'm out of it." Later he said that he wished he had more friends. Most of his free time was spent building models and skiing whenever he could. Also, he worked a paper route, mowed lawns, and did odd jobs. He was quite proud of the fact that he had earned enough money to buy a power lawnmower and thus increase his earnings substantially.

Mr. and Mrs. W. seemed to feel that Kevin had little confidence in himself. He was "always slow to start—then zip." He was small and not very athletic. Some problems in social adjustment showed up in his early school history. "He was too articulate," said Mr. W.

"He made the other kids feel stupid. He became their punching bag." The W.'s felt that some of Kevin's trouble was due to the extensive travel associated with Mr. W.'s work, a great source of tension between them. Mr. W. felt Kevin spent too much time with his mother and needed more masculine influence. Mrs. W., angry and depressed because of her husband's absences, spent much of her energy doing things with Kevin. They both agreed that boarding school would be good for the boy. "But we do worry about drugs, if he's away at a school . . . with all the pressures to use them. He really shouldn't be at a school with lots of sophisticated kids from New York City."

At our first meeting, Kevin said that he had never used any drugs. "I'm not even thinking about it." Several months later I asked him to participate in this study. At that time he was still a nonuser.

Kevin said that drugs were easy to get around school, though no one had ever offered him any. When I asked him why he had never tried marijuana, he replied matter-of-factly, "I don't know. I guess I don't see the point in it . . . I don't see any reason to try. I could get drunk and be safer. Then if I were caught by my parents or the police, it wouldn't be so bad." Kevin's reasons for not doing marijuana were different from those for hard drugs. With marijuana his first worry was getting caught. Health was the least consideration. With more potent drugs his "worry hierarchy" was reversed.

In spite of his definitive "no-point-in-it" stand, Kevin said that he has thought about trying marijuana. "I'm not even considering hard drugs. But sometimes I just think I'd like to do marijuana." In response to my question about whether or not he would try marijuana if it were offered to him at a party, Kevin replied, "I'm not sure. It would depend on the party. If it were at a kid's house, then probably not. But if it was in the woods, I might think about it."

It seemed unlikely to me that Kevin would try marijuana. He was too isolated socially to be offered any, too shy and scared to seek it out, and terrified of being caught.

Mark

Mark was 14 and repeating eighth grade when we first met. He had been in trouble with the police a few months before for shoplifting.

Moreover, he was doing poorly in school. The N.'s thought Mark should go to private school "so he can get some better motivation. He's not doing anything. He's openly against doing schoolwork and against our values. His teachers have given up on him." Mark was dead set against private school. "The trouble with me is I just don't do the work. I do some of the homework and forget about the rest."

He much preferred to spend his time hanging around with his friends. Team sports did not interest him much. The only school activities in which he participated were band and orchestra. He loved playing the trombone. His only passing grade so far that year was in music. Outside of school, Mark was an explorer scout.

Mr. and Mrs. N. had six children; Mark was the oldest. Mr. N. was a professional; Mrs. N. was busy at home with the children. The N.'s were ambitious, hard-working people. Mr. N. had spent eight years getting his bachelor's degree at night. They simply could not understand Mark. "Unfortunately, we're not very close," acknowledged Mr. N. "I'm only close to my work." Mrs. N. exclaimed, "If only I could understand him. There really must be a generation gap. I can't understand his lack of drive. He likes to float. He doesn't even have strong likes or dislikes. Mark sees no future in this world."

While the N.'s seemed to be quite disgusted with Mark, many of their observations remained untainted. Like many young adolescents, Mark had no goals, no special interests and no special talents. He was a poorer-than-average student who had "always hung on by the skin of his teeth." His parents were strict and unbending, having learned from their experience that the "straight and narrow" was the best path. Mark just seemed to drift through each day—doing or not doing as the spirit moved him. He had never taken any drugs, but "I'm thinking about it."

Almost a year later, Mark was still "thinking about it." Drugs were easy to get at school or in Cambridge, but no one had ever offered him any. Most of the students he hangs around with used marijuana once in a while—"maybe once a week." They also drank on weekends. Mark would join them sometimes and get drunk "whenever I get the chance."

Mark does not use any drugs simply because he is afraid of getting caught and "getting a record." He knows some students who have been caught and expelled from school, fears that and his parents' reaction. "If I got in trouble with the police they'd leave me there

—just for a couple of nights." "But I'm still thinking about smoking pot some time." "Would you take it at a party, if someone offered it to you?" I asked. "It would depend on where the party was and who the person was . . . If I never saw the person before I wouldn't take it. A few weeks ago a guy gave my best friend some hash. It wasn't any good—just pine sap and pepper. He wasn't afraid that the "stuff" would hurt him, he just didn't want to get gypped."

No one is pressuring Mark to use drugs. A 15-year-old friend he was staying with during the summer "wouldn't let me." Mark said his friend got stoned a lot (on mescaline). "He keeps saying 'don't try it—isn't good for you." Mark seemed to get a vicarious pleasure out of seeing his friends stoned. He said he thought it was "funny . . . they kept saying that the leaves in the trees looked like faces . . . the stoned guys were howling . . . seeing them like that didn't scare me . . . I had a blast."

Mark certainly prided himself on "doing his own thing." Yet his greatest worry was being totally independent. "I worry about when I get older and leave my parents." This kind of ambivalence around the issue of dependence vs. independence is a major concern of every adolescent. Successful resolution of the conflict in favor of some sort of "healthy" independence is, in my view, one of the most crucial tasks of adolescence.

It was plain that Mark saw nothing wrong with marijuana. He distinguished it from other drugs that he said were bad. He thought "people who took those were dumb . . . they'll ruin you." But marijuana was different. It was safe, if only he could be certain he would never get caught.

Lenny

Lenny was on the verge of tears during most of our first interview. It was the end of the school year and it was questionable whether or not he would pass and be promoted to ninth grade. "I'm here to figure out why I'm doing so bad in school . . . guess I'm lazy." Lenny had always been an average student in his tough suburban school system. But lately he had been getting into trouble—skipping class, talking back, "being an itch," said his guidance counselor. And his grades had dropped substantially. While his parents were not anxious to send him to private school, Mrs. Z. felt the junior and senior high schools were not structured enough. "They simply don't demand anything . . . so he does nothing.'' Lenny did not want to go to private school, but knew ''It depends upon what happens here.''

Mr. and Mrs. Z. were both achievement-oriented. They valued ''consistent work habits, not necessarily the grade.'' Mr. Z was a professional and Mrs. Z. worked part-time doing secretarial work. Both were active in community affairs. Mrs. Z. said she was ''obsessed with school'' and school politics; Mr. Z., in addition to political and professional affairs, was a Little League coach. There were two other children in the family, both younger than Lenny.

Most of our first meeting's conversation focused on school. Lenny was discouraged about how the year had gone. Summer school ''would just wreck my summer.'' He said he would much rather hang around with his friends. He had a job and, furthermore, his family planned a trip to Europe for three weeks. Lenny had a lot of friends. ''I wish I had less sometimes . . . then when I want to be with just one I wouldn't have to say 'get lost.''' Most of his free time was spent ''hanging around'' with kids his age and playing sports. In contrast to Lenny's statements, the Z.'s saw Lenny basically as a ''loner.'' ''He's never had many friends.''

The Z.'s, Mrs. Z. especially, were concerned about the level of Lenny's school performance. Mrs. Z. frankly admitted that she nagged him constantly about his homework. ''We both yell a lot. I always have to remind him—about everything. Something goes wrong every day. We really don't know what to ignore.'' Lenny felt his parents were always ''bugging'' him. ''My father wants things done at a minute's notice. He teases me—'How are your grades doing, Lenny—probably Fs, huh?''' He said his mother was always pestering him. ''She wants me to do work when I have none. I get so mad, I tell her I have none when I do.''

Lenny had always been a difficult child. Very young, he cried a lot and hardly slept. Mrs. Z. felt unsure of herself as a mother and the Z.'s were living far from family supports at the time. Until 11, he was enuretic. Mainly, though, the Z.'s wanted him to do better, and, more importantly, work harder in school. It was clear to me that Lenny felt he could never measure up to their high expectations. He did not think he was good enough in anything.

When I asked him about drugs, Lenny replied, ''Not a chance —not gonna stick a needle in me.'' ''What about marijuana?'' I asked. ''I don't even know what it looks like.''

Like all of the others, Lenny said he knew where he could get drugs if he wanted them, but he did not want them. ''Me and my friends stay away from them. We don't hang around with kids who take them.'' In contrast to Kevin and Mark, Lenny was not thinking about using drugs, not even marijuana. If someone offered him some at a party, he said, ''I'd get the hell out of there. . . It's too risky, you know to your health and with the law . . . You could get all messed up. The kids at our school who take it used to be good kids—Now they act 'turned off'—they hang around with hippies and those faggots with the beads and capes. They look like morons. They do it to be cool. Maybe they can't get off it. I think they're all screwed up . . . fairies saying the world is beautiful and then they walk in front of a car and get squashed like a peanut.''

Besides being turned off by the drug users he knows, Lenny has taken his parents' advice to heart. ''They say drugs can hurt you. Life becomes like a spy operation—You have to first get them; smuggle them into the house; hide them and take care not to get caught. For what? To die at an early age? I want to live long!''

Now you have met the children. In their own words, they have talked about their drug experience or told us why they have chosen not to use drugs. In some ways the users and nonusers are alike. In the next chapter we shall explore the similarities and differences between and within these two groups.

Notes

1. Howard S. Becker article in David Solomon, ed., *The Marihuana Papers,* New York: New American Library, 1966.

2. Richard Goldstein, *1 in 7: Drugs on Campus,* New York: Walker & Co., 1966.

5 Findings

The interviews with each child, as we have seen, are very revealing. Let us now put them together to see what general findings emerge. The data obtained are descriptive and thus, I expect, will begin to provide some clinical understanding of the many statistical findings summarized earlier in Chapter 2. My study was undertaken to probe in some depth how a group of young adolescents confront the issues surrounding drug use. For each of the following categories I will first discuss variables differentiating users from nonusers; nondistinguishing variables follow.

The categories are:

1. Family background variables
2. School variables and attitude toward achievement
3. Interpersonal relationships with peers
4. Interpersonal relationships with family
5. Testing variables
6. Drug intervention exposure and attitudes toward legalization
7. Miscellaneous

Family Background Variables

Difference Between Users and Nonusers

Family intactness distinguished the two groups. All of the nonusers came from intact families, while three out of five users came from families in which there had been at least one divorce.

The parents of each child were asked about outside activities that "consume a substantial amount of your time." The two groups differed in terms of the mothers' reported activities. All of the nonusers' mothers were actively engaged in pursuits outside the home—travel, sports, League of Women Voters, school and community politics, Scouts, and Red Cross. Two out of five mothers of users had no special interests whatever; the rest engaged in home-based activities, such as reading and weaving.

I felt intuitively after preliminary interviewing that in many ways the young people who used drugs felt unloved. They conveyed a lack of self-esteem and an uncertainty about their worthwhileness to others as they spoke. In fact, in both groups all of them seemed to take a great deal of criticism, mainly from their parents and teachers. While I found little difference between the two groups with respect to the quantity of criticism they endured, the quality of it varied. The users seemed to get more *personal* criticism. It seemed as though they were being told almost daily that *they* were bad, defective, or inadequate, rather than that they had done something wrong. In every case, hair and dress were major sources of contention in the users' families. Four out of five users reported frequent criticism about their appearance. "Look how grubby she is," said Barbara's mother to a friend as Barbara came into the room. "They just care about their reputation, so if I look grubby they get upset," complained Ellen. The fifth user reported that his parents gave up criticizing him about his dress and hair. Criticism in the nonusers' families was more diversified, ranging from none to reminders of chores undone and grades lower than expected.

All of the users felt that "Kids my age should be able to decide more things on their own." They felt that their parents should not try to run their lives vis-à-vis their choice of friends, where they went, the hours they kept, what clothes they bought, and (in two cases) whether or not they took drugs. Ellen summed it up best with her statement: "My mother wants me to be what she was—a good and obedient little girl." Of the nonusers, only Mark agreed with the users about this issue. Both Kevin and Lenny felt they had enough decision-making responsibility; they felt that kids their age needed some limits.

No Difference Suggested

As expected, no differences were found between the users and nonusers with respect to age, educational background, and occupation; nor were there differences in levels of achievement, i.e., how well they did in school. In contrast to the finding that the mothers' spare time activities differentiated the two groups, the fathers' outside activities did not seem to matter.

The children were asked about the importance of religion to themselves and to their families. Without exception, each one reported that the practice of his religion was unimportant to him. While six out of eight attend church or synagogue fairly regularly, or at least on major holidays, they say they do so because they have to or because they are required to by school regulations. Lenny summed up the feelings of many of the others as well as his own when he said, "My religion is not important at all—What did Moses ever do for me anyway?" There was a great deal of variability in how divisive an issue religion was in all of the families. These findings seem to be in marked contrast to those of Richard Blum et al.[1] who found that heavy users and nonusers tended to be more interested in religion than moderate users.

I asked these young people how they felt about their upbringing. Was it "too strict" or "too loose?" As I expected, more than half felt that their upbringing was too strict, that rules in their homes were too rigid and punishment too severe.

It's much too strict. . . . They're always saying you better do this or that. . . . I don't do it just to spite them. . . . Discussion and reasoning don't help. . . . They are "the Law."[a]

My parents baby me too much. . . . They're very over-protective, mostly my mother. She thinks of the weirdest things that might happen.[b]

In some cases sneaking was necessary, but there was no difference between the two groups, except for sneaking to use drugs.

One area in which I found Blum's findings most provocative was "family medicating habits." The data on this variable were not readily available, so I had to rely on the child's report of his parents' habits. Most kids could only guess whether or not their parents took medication regularly, what kind, and for what condition. The majority reported that their parents were slow or average in giving them medicines, except for aspirin, which all used freely. Thus no differences between the groups, based on these secondary reports, emerged.

[a]Interview with Paul.

[b]Interview with Lenny.

School Variables and Attitudes Toward Achievement

Difference Between Users and Nonusers

While it may well be an accident of sampling, I found that the users (four out of five) attended private day and boarding schools. All the nonusers, in contrast, attended suburban public schools.

In the previous chapter, many of the drug users were quoted about their school progress. Four out of five users reported doing better in school since the period of drug use had begun. However, no one mentioned a causal relationship between drug use and grades. The nonusers' grades remained at average or below average level.

No Difference Suggested

The two groups seemed to concur about the school subjects they liked best. This finding stands in stark contrast to the college student studies by Blum,[2] who found that users tended to major in humanities and social sciences, while nonusers preferred the more quantitative and scientific fields. Within the user group, I found, as did Blum, that three out of five young people reported their strongest interests were English, humanities, and writing.

All but one of the children reported that they were generally satisfied with school—with *their* school, in particular, and how it was run. Not surprisingly, however, all could suggest ways to change this school. These results are in direct opposition to Robert C. Petersen's[3] hypothesis: that satisfaction with other activities implies less likelihood of finding *regular* drug use appealing. Of course, there were other activities in the lives of each of these young people, but none nearly so time-consuming as school.

The users and nonusers were alike in feeling frustrated with their school performances. However, within the user group, the heaviest users (Ellen, Paul, and Barbara) all were satisfied with their grades. None of them felt thwarted about his level of achievement, whereas Randi and Tom (the occasional users) and the nonusers felt dissatisfied.

I asked each child whether he agreed or disagreed with the statement: "It is important to work hard in school." Then I asked how he thought his parents, individually, would respond. There was no difference between the two groups on this issue. They all agreed that hard work is important, even though they felt that what they were learning had little or no future relevance. Nor was there disagreement within families.

All eight subjects believed that grades were not particularly important. Instead, they emphasized the importance of trying, doing your best, and learning a lot. However, they all shared the common feeling that their parents attached too much importance to specific grades.

Interpersonal Relationships with Peers

Difference Between Users and Nonusers

Interestingly enough, "age of friends" differentiated the two groups quite sharply. All the users report having older friends, whereas all the nonusers' friends are roughly their own age. Only Randi (an occasional user) said that she also had friends her own age. Every user said that his friends used drugs at least as frequently as he. Only one of the nonusers had drug-taking friends.

I found a dramatic, though not unexpected, difference between the two groups with respect to offers of drugs. All the users were offered drugs by friends and others. The nonusers had *never* been offered drugs by anyone.

No Differences Suggested

There were no differences between the two groups in number of friends; desire for more friends; existence of a best friend; and friends' drinking and smoking habits. I had expected to find differences between the groups concerning the desire to join a particular crowd. Surprisingly, there were none.

Interpersonal Relationships with Family

Difference Between Users and Nonusers

Each child was asked about his relationship with his mother. Was it close? Affectionate? Were positive comments made? Four out of five users reported poor relationships with their mothers and testified that little affection, either physical or verbal, was expressed. Several comments are illustrative:

Our relationship is absolutely terrible. Every time we talk we disagree. Then the yelling starts and I end up walking out of the room. It's always been terrible.[c]

It's an unrealistic relationship. Now it's an acting-type relationship —because of drugs. We used to be close until fourth grade when my schoolwork started going down. Then she got colder and colder.[d]

I found no particular pattern in the mother-child relationships of the nonusers. They had more difficulty than the users articulating the nature of their relationship.

No Difference Suggested

The quality of relationships between the children and their fathers in my sample is essentially uncorrelated with drug use. Fathers were perceived as generally less close and less affectionate than mothers. Only one child reported any consistency in receiving positive comments.

In spite of the seemingly poor mother-child and indifferent father-child relationships, these young adolescents had a surprising degree of trust in their parents. There were, however, some times in which the children believed their parents stretched the truth. Both groups believed that their parents would be willing to stand by them "no matter what." Only one child from each group felt his parents would not support him if he were in some sort of serious trouble.

An interesting question is what effect, if any, older siblings have on their brothers' and sisters' decisions to use drugs. Unfortunately,

[c]Interview with Ellen.

[d]Interview with Paul.

since four of the eight young people were either the oldest child or had no siblings, my sample did not really lend itself to explorations in this area.

Testing Variables

In examining the findings in light of several testing variables we can obtain some important clinical impressions of young teenagers. For all users the psychological testing occurred prior to the time that their drug-taking was heaviest. Therefore we really cannot hypothesize about a user personality and the limited sample size precludes any reliable predictions about who will or will not be likely to use drugs. Nevertheless, in the section to follow I present data on the eight young people. While I have tried to minimize the use of psychological jargon throughout this presentation, it is virtually impossible to do so in reporting projective (Rorschach and TAT) test results. The discussion will therefore be of value primarily to readers familiar with psychological testing.

Difference Between Users and Nonusers

Every child took the Rorschach Inkblot Test. A slight evidence of difference in the mean form level ($F\%$) was found between the two groups. The user mean was 47 percent; the nonuser mean was 57 percent. While these results are clearly not significant in a statistical sense, they may suggest that nonusers are somewhat more constricted or inhibited than users.

In addition, there seems to be a noteworthy difference between the two groups in the number of human movement (M) scores produced. The mean M for users was 2.9, almost twice that of nonusers, 1.5. This finding contrasts with that of James H. Kleckner[4] who found that college student users have less ego strength than nonusers.

Unlike many techniques, the Rorschach provides us with a test stimulus that remains essentially constant throughout the entire age span. Louise B. Ames et al., in their well-known book *Adolescent Rorschach Responses,* have gathered a great deal of developmental data on children, ages 2 to 16. This information provides us with an illuminating background against which to view these findings.

The combination of higher *F%* and lower *M* in the nonusers may be indicative of immaturity in that we know that *F%* decreases and *M* increases with age. It is generally agreed that a desirable *F%* in an adult record is 50 percent or below. While Ames cautions that we cannot assume that the nonusers are *highly* constricted in emotional expression if their *F%* is greater than 50 percent, we can say that the users' Rorschach records are more congruent with adult expectations. The same is true with respect to *M* scores. According to Ames' norms, our users' mean *M* is at age level, while the nonusers seem surprisingly young, psychologically speaking. From a developmental-stage viewpoint then, we might hypothesize that the users seem more like middle-stage adolescents. The nonusers appear to have less ego strength to dare to do something unconventional.

Each child was also given 10 cards of the Thematic Apperception Test (TAT) in the standard administration, and the Visual Impressions Test (VIT), a written form which consists of five of the original TAT pictures. The content of the VIT and TAT stories cannot really be analyzed objectively. My aim in this analysis, however, was to see if any themes recurred within each group. There is some evidence to suggest that users trust other people less than nonusers. This was shown most dramatically by four out of five users telling stories in which "people disappoint you," in which people are seen as unreliable, use each other, or want to get something from each other. There was no substantial difference between the groups in frequency of themes involving issues of competence, independence, family relationships, need for acceptance, and the world's predictability.

No Difference Suggested

Everyone was given the Wechsler Intelligence Scale for Children. The mean scores for the nonusers were: Verbal IQ—108, Performance IQ—102, Full-Scale IQ—102. The mean scores for the users were: Verbal IQ—113, Performance IQ—108, Full-Scale IQ—114. Thus the users had slightly higher IQs on average. The individual subtest scores yielded no substantial differences between the two groups. These scores can be found in Appendix B.

The childrens' files contained results of the Cooperative Reading Test (one subject had taken the reading section from the Sequential Tests of Educational Progress, a comparable reading achievement test). A comparison of public school percentiles was made for the two groups. The mean score for nonusers was 83 (percentile), the mean for the users was 85 (percentile). No difference is suggested.

There were also no group differences in level of math achievement. Everyone took the STEP (Sequential Tests of Educational Progress) mathematics section. The mean public school percentile for nonusers was 77, while the mean for users was 83.

Earlier I mentioned some aspects of the Rorschach test scores which distinguished the two groups. While there was no difference between the groups in $M:Fm + m$, there was a great deal of variation in this ratio within the groups. I had anticipated that as a measure of anxiety, $M:Fm + m$ probably would show that users were generally more tense than nonusers, and that we might then hypothesize that drug use plays some role in reducing anxiety. This simply was not the case.

The ratio $M:\Sigma C$ results were also not what I would have guessed. While it could be argued from the literature that users would be generally more introversive than nonusers, it seemed to me that as a group, the users, would be more extratensive—more given to "acting out" conflict in various ways, rather than internalizing it. Once again, I did not find any difference between the groups. There was a great deal of variation *within* each group, which suggests that drug use does not mean the same thing to each person. A hypothesis here is that people who are prone to act out have a good chance of getting around to using drugs. The introversive types may also use them to enhance the process of introspection.

There were no substantial disparities between the two groups on any of the Rorschach dimensions shown in Table 5-1.

Drug Intervention: Exposure and Attitudes Toward Legalization

Difference Between Users and Nonusers

We talked a lot about what, if anything, these young people thought

Table 5-1
Rorschach Scoring Categories

1. Location Scores

Mean Scores

	User Mean	*Nonuser Mean*
W%	59	54
D%	32	35
d%	6	5

2. Total Number of Responses (R)
   User $\bar{X} = 16$
   Nonuser $\bar{X} = 20$

3. Form Level ($F + \%$)
   User $\bar{X} = 87$
   Nonuser $\bar{X} = 85$

4. Popular Responses ($P\%$)
   User $\bar{X} = 31$
   Nonuser $\bar{X} = 24$

5. Animal Responses ($A\%$)
   User $\bar{X} = 52$
   Nonuser $\bar{X} = 51$

should be done to try to prevent others from taking drugs. Six of the eight felt that *something* should be done. When I inquired, "What will work?" the two groups differed sharply in their responses. All nonusers felt that seeing addicts at their worst (not when they have already "kicked" the habit), and people their age who were hospitalized because of drug misuse, would be effective in dissuading many young people from taking drugs.

Taking kids to a jail or hospital and seeing someone coming down from a bad trip or in jail where it's lousy—that would have more effect than TV programs and school assemblies. . . . They should show what drugs do to you—like make you sick or jump out of a window—not just the good parts of being high.[e]

The users' responses were varied. Two kids "really don't know" and believe that "everyone's already made up their mind." Two others think that realistic factual programs, which show both sides of the issue without taking a position, would be most effective.

---

[e]Interview with Kevin.

Barbara believes nothing should be done since "Nothing will work anyway. If you tell kids drugs are bad, they'll try them anyway just to see."

In addition to discussing drug intervention programs, we talked at length about whether or not drugs, particularly marijuana, should be legalized. *All* the users agreed that the sale and use of marijuana should be legal. The three heaviest users, Ellen, Randi, and Barbara, thought that hashish and mescaline should also be legally available. Barbara felt *all* drugs should be legal. The users' reasons were varied.

If they were legal a lot of people wouldn't use them . . . A lot of people are just doing it to revolt against something. . . . Besides it's not such a bad thing.[f]

I don't think it's dangerous. Besides it's ridiculous not to be legal since everyone does it anyway.[g]

When used correctly it [marijuana/mescaline] can be used as a tool to learn and for pleasure. . . . People should be able to make a free choice as long as it doesn't interfere with others.[h]

The nonusers opposed the legalization of all drugs. While they agreed that "nothing was proven yet" about marijuana, they tended to consider any drug a health risk. The users made careful and elaborate discriminations among various drug substances in terms of their potential harmfulness.

There was no difference between the two groups in the feelings about legalizing harder drugs, (anything more potent than marijuana). Seven out of eight children agreed that drugs other than marijuana (hashish and mescaline, in two cases) should *not* be legalized. The nonusers did not distinguish between marijuana and other substances (except for heroin) in citing their reasons against legalization. The users did, and here are some examples of their thinking:

The others (excluding marijuana, hashish, and mescaline) are sort of damaging—you know, to your brain cells. Your over-all thinking recedes if you use too much. . . . Anyway, if a few things are legal and available, that's enough.[i]

[f]Interview with Barbara.

[g]Interview with Randi.

[h]Interview with Paul.

[i]Interview with Paul.

Maybe acid and stuff shouldn't be legal . . . Harm can come, but it's enjoyable . . . [you] can have a bad time. It can damage you emotionally. Like a girl I know—she took four tabs and strangled a cat because it wouldn't come to her. Now she worries about loss of control and that she'll hurt someone.[j]

Clearly, the users' thinking about marijuana contrasted with the nonusers. They viewed it as essentially harmless, physiologically *and* psychologically.

Without exception, these young people had been exposed to a wide gamut of drug intervention programs—films, television, talks by professionals and former addicts. Most of then had experienced several forms of anti-drug campaigning. They *all* agreed that these programs were "not very good, a flop, a waste of time, stunk." Within the nonuser group, two were fascinated by the presentations of ex-addicts. Ironically, the young people felt that the reformed men presented an enticing view of the drug world.

You know seeing those guys doesn't persuade kids not to use drugs. It makes them want to see if it's true—what they say—or what it's really like.[k]

Hearing those ex-junkies talk about how great it was being freaked out —not how it was getting caught or getting off the stuff—I almost considered taking something after that.[l]

Miscellaneous Variables

Differences Between Users and Nonusers

The two groups differed in their use of alcohol. Everyone had taken a drink at one time or another. And, like Blum,[5] I found that more than half of them had been given their first drink by a parent. The users simply drank more often. Reports ran from occasionally, to regularly, to every day. The nonusers rarely took a drink; only one of them had ever been drunk, and then only once; whereas four out of five users drank in order to get drunk. Paul reported having been drunk "more than 50 times." Barbara got drunk a lot; she was

[j]Interview with Ellen.

[k]Interview with Mark.

[l]Interview with Kevin.

drinking every day. Randi and Ellen had been drunk at least six times.

No Difference Suggested

In a number of disparate areas I found no difference between the groups:

They used cigarettes with similar frequency. Essentially they seemed to enjoy doing similar things in their spare time—being with friends, listening to music, and playing sports.

They all felt that others their age should earn some of their own spending money: there was no substantial difference between the groups in terms of jobs held and wages earned.

I wondered about these young adolescents, and asked them whether or not there are any people (personal acquaintances or well-known figures) whom they really admired. Did they have any heroes? To my surprise most of the subjects seemed to have a hard time with this question. If they did admire someone, they could rarely explain why. The spectrum of answers included "no one, some people my own age who seem well-adjusted, Joplin, Ghandi, Freud, and Darwin."

And, finally, in contrast to the findings of Walters' et al.,[6] there was no difference between the two groups in regard to visits to a therapist.

These, then, are the findings. In the next chapter I shall attempt to connect them and discuss their meaning.

Notes

1. Richard Blum, and Associates, *Students and Drugs*, San Francisco: Jossey-Bass, Inc., 1969.

2. Ibid.

3. Robert C. Petersen, "Marihuana and Health—The American Cannabis Research Program," *Mental Health Digest* 3(12) (December 1971).

4. James H. Kleckner, "Personality Differences Between Psychedelic Drug Users and Non-Ususers," *Psychology* 5(2) (1968).

5. Richard Blum and Associates, *Students and Drugs*.

6. Paul A. Walters, Jr., George W. Goethals, and Harrison G. Pope, Jr., "Drug Use and Life Style Among 500 College Undergraduates," *Archives General Psychiatry* 26 (1972).

6

Discussion

I have learned considerably more about young adolescents and drugs than I knew at the outset of this project. While the nature of the sample precludes statistical generalizations, the intensive case studies lead me to some general clinical impressions about marijuana as a psychological phenomenon in the life of a young teenager.

I was surprised to find that for this group of teenagers, initial drug use is more a function of chance than of planning, a fact increasingly clear to me as I continue to work with young people. These children did not go through a series of logical steps to decide to smoke pot. Their first drug experience occurred, rather, because they were curious and because they happened to be with someone who offered them some marijuana. The first drug experience usually began with receiving marijuana free from a friend or sibling who was more experienced.

Drugs seem to be available easily to those who want them. And money is not an issue. Either the youngster has money to finance his experimentation or he makes an easy alliance with someone who will simply give him drugs "cuz he's my friend."

While initial use was motivated primarily by curiosity ("to find out what everyone is talking about"), other reasons determined continued marijuana use and an expansion of the drug repertoire. For the most part, children continued to use marijuana because they liked its effect. It made them feel good and enjoy things more. Unlike college students, the young users do not seem to take drugs for their ritualistic aspects.

We also discover that drug use by young adolescents is a group phenomenon rather than an individual experience. And the fact of the "groupness" is important in perpetuating use. For these young people, much of the appeal of drug-taking stems from the interpersonal elements of the experience. There really does not seem to be a strong association between a particular mood, mental "set" or psychological condition and occasional marijuana use. Nevertheless, a few also use drugs for reasons somewhat analogous to those

71

shared by alcohol users: to facilitate interpersonal interaction. To the extent that the youngsters feel more competent interpersonally, drugs (other than marijuana) seem less important.

Many group activities, it seems to me, provide a way to ward off feelings of loneliness, isolation, and alienation or estrangement. Witness the children of the "Woodstock Nation." They were pressed so closely together that physical movement was almost impossible; yet, truly intimate relationships (in the mature, psychological sense) were not achieved. In fact, my own clinical observations of these and other young adolescents lead me to believe that the quality of friendship is very different for young people today than it was a generation ago. Intimacy, in an Eriksonian sense, has almost vanished. Young adolescents share events and experiences, but rarely each other.

In contrast to the many studies of college students who use drugs heavily (the heads), we learn that younger users, even heavy users, are not part of a drug culture. True, they are part of the youth culture and identify with their age group in terms of dress, hair style, values, and so on. But the heavy users do not identify with so-called heads in terms of life-style. Except for Barbara, they lead essentially straight lives. Drug use for young people this age does not seem to predict anything about life-style. We really cannot separate the users from the nonusers merely by observing them.

In spite of the easy access to a broad range of drug substances, we see that the heavy users do not appear to be in any present danger of using harder drugs. What seems to differentiate them from heads are their friends and their views of themselves. In general, they seem to identify much more with the straight world and with conventional patterns rather than with a drug subculture.

What can we say about the nonuser group? It seems obvious that their nonuse does not stem from an organized system of moral or philosophical beliefs. Instead, they eschew drugs because of the health and legal hazards involved, and for the time being, they see no point or have no reason to. Their convictions (except for Lenny's) are not very firm, as the dialogue in Chapter 4 suggests. In fact, Kevin and Mark say they are "thinking about it." But the general impression we get of these children is that they are more cautious, more inhibited, and also less confident of their ability not to get caught.

The group phenomenon affects the nonusers as it does the users. Not only have they not been offered drugs; their friends do not use them either. Since initial use seems almost accidental, very much a function of associations as well as situations, it seems likely that some proportion of nonuse in this age group is also accidental. While we found a number of differences between users and nonusers, *the major factor differentiating the two groups is that users have been given the chance to use*.

There are a number of respects in which family variables differ between the two groups. Associated with nonuse we find intact families, mothers who are active outside the home, and better relationships between mother and child. While criticism is frequent in all of these families, the users' mothers were especially harsh and rejecting in their disapproval and made few positive statements to their children. There is manifestly some similarity between the family background themes I found and those of alienated youth described by Kenneth Keniston[1] and Harrison Pope.[2] These authors described mother-child relationships that they saw as too close, too sheltered, too dominating, and, thus, not allowing the child to grow up completely. Although Keniston and Pope were describing older adolescents, we can see, though perhaps not quite so vividly, these same qualities in the users' mothers. Essentially their lives revolved around home and children. With nothing to draw their psychic energy away from the family, they had overly invested themselves in making sure their children came out "just right." But at the same time the users felt that they were entitled to more decision-making responsibility. It seems to me, then, quite possible that the nature of these relationships requires more dramatic means for loosening the ties. Perhaps, as Pope hypothesized, because of the lack of autonomy they perceived, these young people felt unable to deal with the world on their own, and were unconsciously looking for ways to test their competence. We see that many of them achieve a real sense of accomplishment from coping with a dangerous activity.

I do not wonder that in a social milieu, which provides minimal opportunities to demonstrate competence and autonomy (the family or society at large), other means must and will be found. For many youths using marijuana becomes a way of proving oneself, proclaims that one is both capable and independent. Why need there be a proof through drugs? Probably because, as the National Commission Report suggests, traditional means like athletics and grades demonstrate competence and competence alone. They do not demonstrate autonomy because they are adult-oriented and controlled.

In addition to family variables, we learn that there are differences between the two groups regarding interpersonal relationships with peers. We see quite strikingly in these case studies what theorists have long expounded: that one of the most influential factors in determining behavior among adolescents is peer group influence. Our users' friends were older, thereby exposing them to practices widely engaged in by a more sophisticated age group. Both users and nonusers show us that having drug-taking friends provides the perfect opportunity for the curious. We also see that it is this shared group experience that offers the lonely, shy or socially awkward youth a means of entering a group. But the opportunity must be there; it seems that few of these young people deliberately seek out drugs. Mere chance, being in the right place at the right time, is a crucial determinant.

Users more than nonusers favor legalization of drug substances. This is not astonishing: people generally tend to deny or de-emphasize the potential dangers of many behaviors in which they engage. Adults around these adolescents continue to smoke in spite of the Surgeon General's Report on the hazards of smoking.

The matter of choice is a distinct element as well. The users seem to be more concerned about controlling their own lives, having more decision-making responsibility. The nonusers seem more content to let others set limits for them. Clearly, whether or not to use marijuana is a decision the users feel should be up to them. Besides, as the TAT stories and the interview data suggest, they really do not trust people very much. Why place your fate, then, in the hands of people you do not trust?

As Pope[3] points out, the young adolescent "sees the older generation's hostility toward marijuana as a display of ignorance, of hypocrisy, and perhaps of thinly disguised envy." I am thoroughly convinced that few parents know as much about drugs as their children. The children are aware of this; they feel that their parents are lying when they pronounce dogmatically that "drugs are bad for you." They see parents who have stressed honesty and who, presumably, value education, thereby presenting moral arguments as if they were facts. The children surmise they are being put on and it makes them angry and distrustful. The scare tactics used by the authorities (medical, legal, psychological) in early drug education programs were just that—scare tactics, not truths. As a result, many of these young people felt betrayed. Their parents and others lied, so why should they be believed even now when more about the dangers of drugs *really* is known.

Though we have not directly seen it in these teenagers, we can well believe Pope's observations of the betrayed youth:

He reacts with a stronger alliance to the subculture, and more rapid acceptance of its beliefs and, often, the use of bigger drugs.[4]

We learn in the case studies that drug education programs have failed miserably. The manifold, well-meant approaches used by the media and in school and church groups do not seem to be meeting these adolescents where they are. The children do not perceive such programs as totally honest, either in presenting scientific evidence or in showing the negative side (bad trips, jail) of drug use. We should be most perturbed, I believe, by the nonusers' reactions to the ex-addicts, whose experiences seem glamorous and inviting, instead of repugnant.

Now that we have looked more closely at the salient findings of this study, let us turn to some theoretical formulations which may further our understanding of the phenomenon of marijuana use.

According to Erik Erikson, adolescence activates a "normative identity crisis,"—a time of transition between childhood and adulthood. This is a period which requires of the individual a relinquishing of certain modes of behavior that were appropriate in childhood but which are not congruent with some vague conception of an adult role.

Becoming adult involves, at a minimum, substituting independence for dependence, individual identity for borrowed or assigned identity, and meaningful social relationships with a variety of individuals outside the family circle. . . . It involves development of meaningful sexual identity . . . and a meaningful relationship to life and the meaning of life.[5]

This process requires of the individual not only a reorganization of his interpersonal life and of his concept of self, but also forces him into choices and decisions which are in the nature of life commitments. Simultaneous decision-making in various spheres of life —physical intimacy, education, occupational choice, and the definition of self—is very anxiety-provoking for many teenagers. While the pressure on a young adolescent is often not nearly as intense as it is on late high school and college students, he seems to be aware of both parental and societal expectations and does not want to think about them. He gets the message even if it is an unspoken one. He knows that he is not ready to make difficult, stressful decisions. Our society seems to insist that adolescents resolve all of these issues at once, and this may be demanding too much. An individual must defend himself somehow in the face of conflict and anxiety. But how?

One way, surely, is to look for magical, instant solutions. Through the ages men have relied on magic potions as curative agents. Sidney Cohen says, "During every epoch of discontent, despair, and directionlessness, there have been those who sought the magic of a potion or a prophet that would provide quick answers, easy utopias, or instant surcease."[6] Ours is a pill-taking society. The mass media inform us regularly that we need not endure headache tension, that tired feeling, or feeling tense. They tell us that there is a chemical solution for every ailment; large segments of the American public are conditioned to cope with stress by taking drugs. An affluent and instant society, as well as changes in child-rearing practices, have taught our children that the ability to tolerate frustration and other anxieties is not necessary. We live in a world that has provided our young with immediate gratification and relief.

Thus it is not so startling to find so many children looking to drugs of all sorts as a means of escaping the pressures and substantial tensions of life. Richard Blum called these students the drug optimists. They grew up confident that for every ill there is a drug to cure it. That younger and younger children (especially middle-class children) turn to drugs may well be a natural consequence of the pressures inflicted on them to achieve in school and to make early decisions about their future. These stresses have crept all the way down into the elementary grades. Listening to suburban children talking among themselves or to their guidance counselors affords us many insights into their desire for escape. Carried to an extreme, drug use as an instrument to resolve conflict leads to "dropping out" in its most total form.

Many parents ask me: "Why do kids need to escape now? They didn't used to." That is not really true. Many adults do not realize that only a short time ago children could delay making decisions about the future in an array of socially acceptable ways. Before the

Vietnam War, students knew that they could easily take a year off to "find themselves." Many students even found military service an attractive way of putting off some of the commitments required of them. The Peace Corps, VISTA, the grand tour of Europe, working for a year, all were readily available options for many students to experiment with a repertoire of different roles. These young people could *legitimately* create a time when they could feel unhemmed in by society's demands. Erikson calls this a "psychosocial moratorium" and defines it thus:

A moratorium is a period of delay granted to somebody who is not ready to meet an obligation or forced on somebody who should give himself time. By psychosocial moratorium, then, we mean a delay of adult commitments, and yet it is not only a delay. It is a period that is characterized by a selective permissiveness on the part of youth and yet it also often leads to deep, if often transitory, commitment on the part of youth, and ends in a more or less ceremonial confirmation of commitment on the part of society.[7]

Erikson believes that each society institutionalizes a kind of moratorium for its youth and that these are experiences which are congruent with society's values. I see fewer opportunities for such a moratorium today. What we may be witnessing in many students is, I feel, a desperate attempt at creating for themselves privileged moments, brief moratoria, in which to come to know themselves better so that they can deal with the requirements of adolescence and impending adulthood. In other students we may be seeing the "identity confusion" that Erikson talks about: the psychological state resulting from the pressure by society, family, etc., for a sort of closure at a time when, as immature people, they are simply incapable of making serious commitments. Drugs provide for some students, therefore, a transitory moratorium.

Another fact of the process of normal adolescent growth and development is a reexamination of what were, in preadolescent days, the absolutes. The absolutes for most children are parental attitudes and values, and the beliefs in parental omnipotence and omniscience. Careful scrutiny of these values and attitudes and the questioning or repudiation of them is a natural part of the growth process from childhood to adolescence. Moving away from parents toward peers is another natural consequence. Frequently this move activates a strong desire for membership in a particular circle of peers: the "in group." Drug use often is a vehicle which facilitates entry into that group. It also may reinforce the adolescent's identification with that group.[8]

Frequently the loosening of childhood ties to parents can be facilitated by overt expressions of estrangement from them. Examples are outlandish modes of dress and hair styles, and speech patterns. Historically, we know that adolescent rebellion, effected by engaging in activities frowned upon by one's elders, has always been a facilitator in the process of "subordinating . . . childhood identifications to a new kind of identification."[9] The generation gap is nothing new. There has always been conflict between young and old and youths' battle for recognition has often been waged around prohibited acts or ideas. In the twenties young people were involved with "sex, sin, and bathtub gin"[a]; in the Coolidge era they joined liberal causes. The fifties were a decade of both dropping out and going on the road. Many students headed west in order to "Berkeley it," or to the Village,[b] or became hangers on in Harvard Square. In the sixties they began to "turn on."

Erikson's theory is a general one and, as an instrument for understanding marijuana use, applies not only to the search for identity, but also to the need for peer group acceptance, for a moratorium, and to experience-seeking itself. It provides us with a broad context for inquiring into many aspects of adolescent behavior aside from the use of drugs. Though it does not explain such motives as pleasure-seeking, or enable us to predict who will or will not use drugs, we must not blame Erikson for these omissions. He did not purport to explain drug use. In its orientation, his theory views most behavior in terms of defense mechanisms. People take drugs as a defense against anxiety or some sort of psychologically uncomfortable feelings. He does not regard most behavior in adaptive terms.

In contrast, Paul A. Walters[10] aims to understand marijuana use as both a social phenomenon that tells us something about the culture of the 1960s and also as a developmental issue: it seems to be related to the efforts of young people to solve certain problems in personal growth. He believes that "identity formation depends more on the ability to respond to most internal and external demands

---

[a]This phrase was used by Dr. George Goethals in a lecture at Harvard University.
[b]Greenwich Village in New York.

as opportunities for adaptation. Rather than focusing on drugs as a defensive device against internal problems in an individual, I would prefer to discuss drug use in relation to areas of adaptation with which it may or not interfere."[11] Walters discusses, in his paper, the attractions of marijuana use to young people: its desired effect on object relations (relationships with others), on cognition, and on the self-image and ego ideal (the internal structures of the psyche).

Although he is obviously talking about older adolescents, especially students in college, I believe Walters' formulations concerning object relations may apply to many early adolescents as well. Most of the eight young people I talked to felt consciously or unconsciously either unloved, or isolated interpersonally, or both. Their *primary* reason for using marijuana did not seem to be to solve problems in object relations. However, they were evidently unhappy about these problems (especially Ellen, Barbara, and Tom), and saw using drugs as a means of making things better. As Walters says:

. . . for many young people, marijuana can be temporarily adaptive by helping them avoid the responsibility of intimacy through the creation of a seemingly intimate group, in which narcissism is a unifying aim. If used temporarily, this device is not likely to interfere with the development of object relationships. If used as a solution to concerns and anxieties about object relationships, it can delay the process of maturation.[12]

Of the aforementioned three students only Barbara seemed to rely on drugs as a near total solution, and her psychological impairment is readily apparent.

Drug-taking certainly may be interpreted as a rebellion against "the logical, goal-oriented, achievement-based secondary process thinking which has been constantly demanded throughout a young person's development."[13] However, I feel it is hard to argue persuasively that this is the major impetus for marijuana use among very young adolescents. Their revolt seems to be more global and ill-defined, lacking the sophistication and finesse more frequently seen in that of college students.

Shall we be alarmed, then, about the upsurge in drug use? The National Commission report concludes:

We believe that experimental or intermittent use of this drug carries minimal risk to the public health and should not be given overzealous attention in terms of a public health response. We are concerned that social influences might cause those who would not otherwise use the drug to be exposed to the minimal risk and the potential escalation of drug-using patterns. For this group, we must deglorify, demythologize and de-emphasize the use of marijuana and other drugs.[14]

Walters says, from an individual psychological perspective:

What drug use indicates is alienation from the current values by which young people are surrounded. Drug use represents a refuge which is half-way between the narcissism of childhood and the adult's mastery of reality. For many young people, the drug experience is an important prelude to maturation. For others, it represents a prolongation of childhood.[15]

Finally, Harrison Pope reminds us:

Drug use ranges from simple fun—a transient relief from boredom—to an entire way of life, an identity which buffers against apathy. . . .[16]

For far too long, generalizations about drug users have given rise to blanket statements and condemnations. Yet after studying these young people intensively, I feel that few absolutes are appropriate. Young people use drugs for a multitude of reasons—some situational, some accidental, some personal.

Adolescence is a difficult stage of life. Major issues beset each youth. *He* knows and *we* know that their manner of resolution will affect the course of his life. The young person must begin to look at himself and try to answer the eternal questions: "Who am I?" and "Where am I going?" Simultaneously, he must frequently deal with group pressure and perhaps an intense sense of isolation and emptiness.

For some youngsters using drugs is clearly a shield against the anxiety these questions generate. Using drugs often leads to abusing drugs in a downhill spiral of self-defeating behavior. For many others, however, drug-taking differs very little from the "few Saturday night beers" of a generation ago.

Notes

1. Kenneth Keniston, *The Uncommitted,* New York: Dell Publishing Co., Inc., 1960.

2. Harrison Pope, Jr., *Voices from the Drug Culture*, Cambridge, Mass: The Sanctuary, 1971.

3. Ibid., p. 86.

4. Ibid., p. 86.

5. Helen Nowlis, *Drugs on the College Campus*, New York: Doubleday-Anchor Books, 1969, p. 21.

6. Sidney Cohen, "The Cyclic Psychedelics," *American Journal Psychiatry* 125 (1968): 393.

7. Erik H. Erikson, *Identity: Youth and Crisis*, New York: Norton & Co., 1968, p. 147.

8. Ernest Harms, ed. *Drug Addiction in Youth*, New York: Pergamon Press, 1965.

9. Erik H. Erikson, *Identity: Youth and Crisis*, p. 154.

10. Paul A. Walters, Jr., "Drugs and Adolescence: Use and Abuse" in *Emotional Problems of the Student*, 2nd ed. Edited by Graham B. Blaine, Jr. and Charles C. McArthur, New York: Prentice Hall, 1971.

11. Ibid., p. 155.

12. Ibid., p. 157-58.

13. Ibid., p. 159.

14. National Commission: *Marihuana: A Signal of Misunderstanding, The Official Report of the National Commission on Marijuana and Drug Abuse*, New York: New American Library, 1972, p. 113.

15. Paul A. Walters, Jr., "Drugs and Adolescence," p. 162.

16. Harrison Pope, Jr., *Voices from the Drug Culture*, p. 121.

Appendixes

Appendix A:
Guide to Interview

Introduction

What do you and people your age seem to enjoy doing most in your spare time?

Are there any people (personal, well-known) whom you really admire?

Amount of money you spend on yourself each week?

> Is that enough?
> Where does it come from?

Should teenagers earn their own money?

Ever saved any money? For what?

How well do you enjoy school? Are you generally satisfied with the way things are run there?

What sorts of things are you dissatisfied with?

Has anyone ever told you that you should be doing better in school? Why?

> Do others criticize you in other ways?
> Is your upbringing too loose or strict—in what ways?
> How important is religion to you? Do you attend church regularly?

Tell me first how you would respond to each of these statements. Then tell me about your mother, then father: how would they respond?

> It is important to work hard in school.
> It is important to get good grades.
> Young people should have to do chores at home.
> My bedtime is reasonable.
> I think my allowance is enough money for someone my age.
> I think children my age should be able to decide more things on their own.
> Going to religious school is worthwhile.
> It is important to go to religious services as often as I do.
> The rules in my house are reasonable.
> Punishments are too strict in my house.
> Hair and dress are issues in our household.

Have you ever had an alcoholic beverage?
>   If yes, where did you have your first drink?
>   Who gave you your first drink?
>   What was it (wine, beer, gin. etc.)?
>   How often do you have a drink?
>   Have you ever been drunk?
>   Do you smoke?

Relationships and Drug Use

Number of people you regularly spend time with?

Their ages?

How many are best friends?

Do you ever wish you had more friends?

The crowd you would like to belong to—what is it like?

Do good friends use drugs/drink/smoke?

Has anyone ever offered you drugs? Who?

Have you ever taken drugs for other than medical purposes? Which ones (list below)?
>   Marijuana
>   LSD (acid)
>   Speed
>   Glue (sniffing)
>   Cough syrup
>   Heroin
>   Sleeping pills
>   Others—please name them.

If you want drugs, can you get them around school?

If you cannot get them around school, where are they available?

If you use drugs, why do you?

If not, why not?

Are you thinking about trying drugs sometime soon?

If you use drugs, what would make you stop?

If you were at a party and a friend offered you marijuana, would you try it? Why/why not?

If not tried, why not (reasoning)? What reasons can you give for it?

If you are thinking about it, why? How do you reason about it?

If you were offered, would you try it? Why? If not, why not? Are you scared? Afraid to get caught?

Would you take it if you were not afraid of being caught?

If it were not illegal?

If you did not have to worry about your health?

You told me you were thinking about taking drugs (if applicable). Why would *you* take them?
> Follow up
> Suggest alternatives

Do you think should be legalized? Should all drugs be legal?
> Why/why not?
> Which ones?
> What about Thalidomide, if student says "all."

How he got started using marijuana (or any other drugs).
> When first use occurred?
> Where?
> With whom, if anyone—how old?
> How drug was obtained?
> What made you decide to use it?
> Major reason for first use?

Description of first experience
> How did it make you feel?
> Compare effect with what expected.
> How you felt about trying it (using it) after that first time?
> What drug did you use?

Pattern of use after first experience.
> Motivation for continuation
> More on what drug does for you

Circumstances in which uses occur.
> Where?
> With whom?
> How often?

Feelings about doing something illegal/frowned on.

Plans for *future* use.
> continue—why?
> stop—why?

What would make you stop or begin to use?

Is life more fun with drugs? Why?

What do you feel are your needs (psychological) to use it or is it a way to have fun?

Feelings about achievement.
> Feelings toward achievement *before* use
> *during*
> after (if stopped)
> i.e., do you notice any change in feelings about school?

Academic performance.
> Any changes in grades over the time drug use occurred (is occurring)?
> Are you frustrated because you are doing poorly in school?
> How relevant is school to life?

Relationship between use and older sibling use.

Medical orientation of family.
> Medicating practices
> Sick often—good/bad

Relationship with mother: how close/affectionate; physical/verbal: does she say "I love you?" Positive comments?

Relationship with father: how close/affectionate; positive comments?

Do you trust them to tell you the truth?

Do you feel parents would stand behind you no matter what you did?

Have you discussed issue of drug use with parents?

What reasons do they give against use? What do you say (or think)?

Do they know extent of use?

How do you hide it?

Sneak in other areas?

What did parents do when they found out (if they know)?

What do you think they would do? (if they do not know)

Ideas and attitudes toward intervention.
     Should anything be done to keep young people from drugs?
     What?
     What have you been exposed to?

Appendix B:
Wechsler Results (rounded to nearest whole)

	Nonusers	Users
Verbal IQ	Mean ($\bar{X}$) = 108 Median (Mdn) = 106	$\bar{X}$ = 113 Mdn = 110
Performance IQ	$\bar{X}$ = 102 Mdn = 101	$\bar{X}$ = 108 Mdn = 106
Full Scale IQ	$\bar{X}$ = 102 Mdn = 102	$\bar{X}$ = 114 Mdn = 111

Subtest

Scaled score means (X)

	Nonusers	Users
Information	14	10
Comprehension	11	10
Arithmetic	8	12
Similarities	14	14
Vocabulary	12	13
Digit Span	9	11
Picture Completion	12	10
Picture Arrangement	10	11
Block Design	11	12
Object Assembly	9	11
Digit Symbol	10	12

Bibliography

Blum, Richard and Associates. *Society and Drugs*. San Francisco: Jossey-Bass Inc., 1969.

Blum, Richard and Associates. *Students and Drugs*. San Francisco: Jossey-Bass Inc., 1969.

Blum, Richard and Associates. *Utopiates: The Use and Users of LSD-25*. New York: Atherton Press, 1964.

Blumer, Herbert. "The World of Youthful Drug Use." Addiction Center Final Report. University of California, at Berkeley, 1967.

Boston Evening Globe. Becker Survey Data, March 16, 1970.

Bowers, Malcolm; Chipman, Abram; Schwartz, Arthur and Dann, O. T. "Dynamics of Psychedelic Drug Abuse." *Archives General Psychiatry* 16 (1967): 560-66.

Cohen, Sidney. "The Cyclic Psychedelics." *American Journal Psychiatry* 125 (1968): 393-94.

Cohen, Sidney. *The Drug Dilemma*. New York: McGraw-Hill, 1969.

DeBold, Richard C. and Leaf, Russell C., eds. *LSD, Man, and Society*. Wesleyan University Press, 1967.

Demos, George and Shainline, John W. "Drug Use on the College Campus: A Pilot Study." unpublished, 1967.

Eells, Kenneth, "A Survey of Student Practices and Attitudes with Respect to Marihuana and LSD." Unpublished, 1967.

Eells, Kenneth. "Marihuana and LSD: A Survey of one College Campus." *Journal of Counseling Psychology* 15(5) (1968): 459-67.

Erikson, Erik H. *Identity: Youth and Crisis*. New York: Norton & Co., 1968.

Farnsworth, Dana. "Drugs—Their Use and Abuse by College Students." in *Psychiatry, Education and the Young Adult*. Springfield, Illinois: Charles C. Thomas, 1966.

Goldstein, Richard. *1 in 7: Drugs on Campus*. New York: Walker and Co., 1966.

Goode, Erich, ed. *Marijuana*. New York: Atherton Press, 1969.

Grinspoon, Lester. "Marihuana." *Scientific American* 221(6), December 1969, 17-25.

Harms, Ernest, ed. *Drug Addiction in Youth*. New York: Pergamon Press, 1965.

Keeler, Martin. "Motivation for Marihuana Use: A Correlate of Adverse Use." *American Journal Psychiatry* 125(3) (1968): 386-90.

Keniston, Kenneth. *The Uncommitted*. New York: Dell Publishing Co., Inc., 1960.

Kleckner, James H. "Personality Differences Between Psychedelic Drug Users and Non-Users." *Psychology* 5(2) (1968): 66-71.

Louria, Donald B. *The Drug Scene*. New York: McGraw-Hill, 1968.

National Commission: *Marihuana: A Signal of Misunderstanding, The Official Report of the National Commission on Marihuana and Drug Abuse*. New York: New American Library, 1972.

Nowlis, Helen. *Drugs on the College Campus*. New York: Doubleday-Anchor Books, 1969.

Nowlis, Helen. "Why Students Use Drugs." *American Journal Nursing* 68 (1969): 1680-85.

McGlothlin, William H. and Cohen, Sidney. "The Use of Hallucinogenic Drugs Among College Students." *American Journal Psychiatry* 122 (1965): 572-74.

McGlothlin, William and West, Louis. "The Marihuana Problem: An Overview." *American Journal Psychiatry* 125(3) (1968): 370-78.

Pearlman, Samuel. "Drug Use and Experience in an Urban College Population." *American Journal Orthopsychiatry* 38(3) (1968): 503-14.

Petersen, Robert C. "Marihuana and Health—The American Cannabis Research Program." *Mental Health Digest* 3(12), December 1971, pp. 13-20.

Pillard, Richard C. "Marihuana." *New England Journal Medicine* 283(6), August 1970, pp. 294-303.

Pope, Harrison, Jr. *Voices from the Drug Culture*. Cambridge, Mass.: The Sanctuary, 1971.

Rosevear, John. *Pot: A Handbook of Marihuana*. New York: University Books, 1967.

Solomon, David, ed. *The Marihuana Papers*. New York: New American Library, 1966.

Sprinthall, Norman A. and Mosher, Ralph L. *Studies of Adolescents in Secondary School.* Cambridge, Mass.: Center for Research and Development on Educational Differences, 1969.

Walters, Paul A., Jr. "Drugs and Adolescence: Use and Abuse." In *Emotional Problems of the Student,* 2nd ed. Edited by Graham B. Blaine, Jr. and Charles C. McArthur. New York: Prentice Hall, 1971.

Walters, Paul, A., Jr.; Goethals, George W.; and Pope, Harrison G., Jr. "Drug Use and Life Style Among 500 College Under-graduates." *Archives General Psychiatry* 26 (1972): 92-96.

Zinberg, Norman. "Facts and Fancies about Drug Addiction." *Public Interest* 6 (1967): 75-90.

Zinberg, Norman. "Narcotics in the U.S.: A Brief History." *Harvard Review.* Summer 1963.

"Marihuana and Society." Prepared by the Council on Mental Health. *Journal American Medical Associtaation* 204(13) (1968): 1181-82.

About the Author

Patricia K. Light received the B.A. from Bennington College and holds the doctorate in psychology from Harvard University. She has been affiliated with the Brookline and Newton, Massachusetts school systems and has served as a Clinical Fellow in Psychology at Massachusetts General Hospital. Dr. Light is now on the staff of the Harvard Graduate School of Business Administration. She was born in 1939 in Elizabeth, New Jersey.

DATE DUE

APR 24 '78	APR 24 '78		
DEC 10 '79	DEC 8 '79		
APR 30 '81	APR 29 '81		
OCT 30 '81	OCT 28 '81		
DEC 10 '81	DEC 8 '81		
AP 28 '86	MAY 5 '86		
DE 4 '87	DEC 8 '87		
GAYLORD			PRINTED IN U.S.A